Algorithmic Trading with Python

Quantitative Methods and Strategy Development

Chris Conlan

Contents

Algorithmic Trading with Python: Quantitative Methods and Strategy Development
Chris Conlan
Bethesda, Maryland
USA

ISBN-13: 979-8-6327-8498-6

About the Author

Chris Conlan is the founder and CEO of Conlan Scientific, a financial data science consultancy based out of Bethesda, Maryland. He works with his team of data scientists to build machine learning solutions for banks, lenders, investors, traders, and fintech companies. Chris graduated University of Virginia's College of Arts & Sciences with a degree in statistics, where he later co-taught a data science capstone course.

Preface

In September of 2016, I published *Automated Trading with R*. My plan, at the time, was to create a starting point for traders hoping to develop and operate automated trading strategies in the R programming language.

The problem with plans is that nothing ever goes according to plan. Me and my small community of readers worked through a lot of hiccups and issues, some of which were out of our control or totally insurmountable. In the end, I am doubtful that anyone really used my platform to do any trading.

The goal of this book is to accomplish what I originally set out to do, but in Python. I will draw from past experiences to create a stable, extensible, and educational book.

0.1 The State of R vs. Python

Having witnessed the feverish adoption of the R programming language at quantitative departments in many universities, I was optimistic that the language itself was on a path towards widespread adoption and expansion. To an extent, it has achieved that. For example, at my alma mater, I see about equal utilization of R and Python in the statistics department. Further, I see R is preferred in life science while Python is preferred in data science.

As of the time of writing in early 2020, Python has solidified itself as the leading language for quantitative trading and financial data analysis. I attribute this to Python's `pandas` and `sklearn` libraries. These two libraries make Python the leader in the machine learning technologies that are most relevant to quantitative trading. As such, the code in this book will be written in Python.

0.2 Lessons Learned from Publishing a Book

I had huge ambitions for *Automated Trading with R* and its evolution within the community. I set up GitHub repos, forum sites, data repos, and blogs. I tried to keep on top of changing packages and API's, and I tried to communicate fixes and changes to my readers. In the end, I couldn't keep up.

0.2.1 Finding a Reliable Data Source

Part of my ambition to create an educational text whose codebase had stability and longevity was to select a reliable API for stock data. As my thinking went, a reliable API would not only place the responsibility for delivering the data on a 3rd party, but it would also ensure that anyone picking up my book in the future would always be working with up-to-date data.

0.2.1.1 Mistakes Made

Most comical among my attempts to support my earlier book were those to replace the ever-changing and ever-deprecating free APIs for end-of-day (EOD) stock data, on which the book depended. My struggle is immortalized in a single blog post, in which I issued over 10 updates over the first year of the book's release, just trying to keep up with which APIs still worked. You can find it here: https://chrisconlan.com/download-daily-data-every-sp-500-stock-r/.

For those who are unfamiliar with the matter, the code in my earlier book pulled EOD price data for over 500 stocks, against which readers would build their automated trading platforms. Shortly after I published the book, the Yahoo Finance API we were using suddenly disappeared and stopped supplying data, effectively ruining the reproducibility of the code at a very early phase.

I won't take total responsibility for Yahoo's decision to take down the API, but I feel partially responsible for encouraging a few thousand people to run these few lines of R code.

```
url <- "http://trading.chrisconlan.com/SPstocks.csv"
stocks_to_load <- as.character(read.csv(url, header=FALSE)[,1])

for ( i in 1:length(stocks_to_load) ) {
    stock_symbol = stocks_to_load[i]
    df <- get_yahoo_finance_data(stock_symbol)
    write.csv(df, file=paste0(stock_symbol, ".csv"))
}
```

Listing 0.1: Partial responsibility

From that point on, the book was very careful and responsible with regards to requesting data from Yahoo Finance, or any API for that matter, but I digress.

0.2.1.2 Nothing is Free

I would not hesitate to say that there are actually less options available to researchers for free EOD stock data than there were 5 years ago. Many sources have come and gone in the time that I have been monitoring this issue. All I can say for sure, is that I won't publish any book that relies on a free API for data.

This book will use strictly fake simulated data, and that data will be available to anyone through the GitHub repository at which the source code is hosted. Anyone with the capability to read and understand the material in this book should be able to substitute in premium data resources with relative ease. With regards to data, this book will prioritize reproducibility over realism.

0.2.1.3 Note on Simulated Data

Some would argue it is a fool's errand to attempt to learn the ropes of algorithmic trading on simulated data. To those critics, I would like to offer two points.

1. Leading quantitative researchers rely on simulated data to backtest their strategies against novel scenarios.
2. The simulated data I've provided is extremely realistic. You might even recognize some of your favorite stocks.

0.2.2 Maintaining a Community

After this book is released, there are bound to be some bugs discovered, and we might have to update some dependencies. My position on this is simple: GitHub Issues is the best place to discuss those things.

We will use GitHub and the GitHub Issues page for the official repository as our primary mode of communication regarding this book and its code. Bug fixes and patches will be made directly on the official GitHub repository.

If any readers opt to set up Reddit or Discord communities to discuss the material, they are welcome to. As the author, I will at least commit to being active and responsive on the book's official GitHub repo.

0.2.3 Publishing

In the past, I have had trouble issuing updates to my books through traditional publishers. I will be self-publishing this book, and it will only be sold online. Critical updates to the content and code will arrive in the form of new editions and updates to the GitHub repository.

0.3 General Changes

This book will have a slightly different focus than *Automated Trading with R.* While the prior book focused heavily on the logistics of building an end-to-end trading platform, this book will forgo those logistical topics to focus on the theory and construction of a simulator and optimizer, with extra care given to how to research new strategic opportunities. This will include a treatment of machine learning and alternative data near the end.

0.4 Acknowledgements

I would like to offer my deepest thanks to everyone that has supported me and my work over the years. I have really enjoyed interacting with and learning from the enthusiastic members of this community. I hope, with the release of this book, we can reignite and continue that relationship.

Chapter 1

Overview

Rather than be a text with code, this book aims to be a text about code. Specifically, this is a book written about a codebase that existed before the book was written. As we navigate the codebase, we will encounter and explore various key aspects of algorithmic trading. Thus, we will start with a brief overview of the codebase.

1.1 Python Conventions

This section will discuss various issues and conventions regarding Python as applied in this book.

1.1.1 Type Hints

Python is a dynamically typed language, which is good for development speed, but bad for readability. I prefer to use type hints when possible to improve readability.

In Python 3.5, the `typing` module was added to the standard library, as well as syntactical support for type hints. A lot of custom Python compilers and IDE's have been released that try to *do* something with these type hints, but standard compilers basically ignore them. They mostly exist for the benefit of developers and future readers of their code.

They better enable developers to write and handle complex data types. For example, I can document the following complex data types as such.

```
from typing import List, Dict, Tuple, Any
import numpy as np
import datetime

# A list of floating point numbers
v: List[float] = [i * 1.23 for i in range(10)]

# A list of mixed type values
v: List[Any] = ['apple', 123, 'banana', None]

# A dictionary of floats indexed by dates
v: Dict[datetime.date, float] = {
    datetime.date.today(): 123.456,
    datetime.date(2000, 1, 1): 234.567,
}
```

```
# A dictionary of lists of strings indexed by tuples of integers
v: Dict[Tuple[int, int], List[str]] = {
    (2, 3): [
        'apple',
        'banana',
    ],
    (4, 7): [
        'orange',
        'pineapple',
    ]
}

# An incorrect type hint
# Your compiler or IDE might complain about this
v: List[str] = [1, 2, 3]

# A possibly incorrect type hint
# There is no concensus on whether or not this is correct
v: List[float] = [1, None, 3, None, 5]

# This is non-descript but correct
v: List = [(1,2,'a'), (4,5,'b')]

# This is more descriptive
v: List[Tuple[int, int, str]] = [(1,2,'a'), (4,5,'b')]

# Custom types are supported
from typing import NewType
StockTicker = NewType('StockTicker', str)
ticker: StockTicker = 'AAPL'

# Functions can define input and return types
def convert_to_string(value: Any) -> str:
    return str(value)
```

Listing 1.1: Type-hinting examples

Throughout this book, I will try to use type hints wherever I feel they can improve understanding of the code for myself and readers. Also, most code examples will assume readers have imported `List`, `Dict`, `Tuple` and `Any` from the `typing` package.

1.1.2 Data Structures and Data Frames

Most of the data we deal with in financial analysis can be reasonably expressed as a *data frame*. From a language-agnostic perspective, data frames are special implementation of a collection of vectors with the following properties.

- Vectors must all be the same length, where one vector constitutes a column. The collection of equal-length vectors creates a table.
- The columns can be of different types, but each column contains data of only one type.
- Both the rows and the columns in of the table are addressable via separates indexes.

These characteristics are present in classes with names like *data frame* or *data table* in a handful of different languages.

1.1.2.1 Pandas Data Frames and Series

The evolution of **pandas** has changed the way quants think about structuring data in recent years. **pandas** offers the **pd.DataFrame** class and the **pd.Series** class, which have capabilities that go above and beyond what is expected of standard data frames.

```
import pandas as pd
import datetime

data = {
    'SPY': {
        datetime.date(2000, 1, 4): 100,
        datetime.date(2000, 1, 5): 101,
    },
    'AAPL': {
        datetime.date(2000, 1, 4): 300,
        datetime.date(2000, 1, 5): 303,
    },
}
df: pd.DataFrame = pd.DataFrame(data=data)
print(df)
# Returns ...
#             SPY  AAPL
# 2000-01-04  100   300
# 2000-01-05  101   303

# Index by column
aapl_series: pd.Series = df['AAPL']
print(aapl_series)
# Returns ...
# 2000-01-04    300
# 2000-01-05    303
# Name: AAPL, dtype: int64

# Index by row
start_of_year_row: pd.Series = df.loc[datetime.date(2000, 1, 4)]
print(start_of_year_row)
# Returns ...
# SPY     100
# AAPL    300
# Name: 2000-01-04, dtype: int64

# Index by both
start_of_year_price: pd.Series = df['AAPL'][datetime.date(2000, 1, 4)]
print(start_of_year_price)
# Returns ...
# 300
```

Listing 1.2: Pandas data types

In the above example, you can see that **pandas** treated the **datetime.date** instances as the row index and the **str** tickers and the column indexes. Then, when a column or row is extracted from the **pd.DataFrame**, it becomes a **pd.Series**, which retains either the column or row index. From here, the **pd.Series** is also indexable.

You can also build a **pd.Series** from a single column and an index.

```
# Create a series
series = pd.Series(data=data['SPY'])
print(series)
# Returns ...
# 2000-01-04    100
# 2000-01-05    101
# dtype: int64
```

Listing 1.3: More pandas data types

1.1.2.2 Time Complexity in Pandas Indexes

It is easy to see why date-indexed series of prices can be useful to quantitative traders. One additional feature of `pandas` data frames and series we should mention, is that they are ordered but set-like. By set-like, I mean that looking up values in them incurs $O(1)$ time complexity, where looking up values in a regular list incurs $O(n)$ time complexity. This feature is key to the speed of many of `pandas`'s in-built functions.

```
dates = [datetime.date(2000, 1, i) for i in range(1, 11)]
values = [i**2 for i in range(1, 11)]
series = pd.Series(data=values, index=dates)

# O(n) time complexity search through a list
print(datetime.date(2000, 1, 5) in dates)
# Returns ...
# True

# O(1) time complexity search through an index
print(datetime.date(2000, 1, 5) in series.index)
# Returns ...
# True
```

Listing 1.4: Pandas indexes

1.1.2.3 Conventions Regarding Vectors and Tables

Throughout this book, we will venture to use `pd.Series` when dealing vectors of financial data, which you can assume will be indexed by `datetime.date` or `datetime.datetime` objects. We will also venture to use `pd.DataFrame` objects whenever dealing with tabular data, which will be similarly date-indexed.

1.1.2.4 Pandas and the Quant Community

Over the years, `pandas` has gotten a lot of love and attention from the quant trading community. As we proceed through this book, you will come across certain `pandas` functions that feel like they were made for nothing but quant trading. This is likely the case, and all the more reason to embrace learning to work with this library.

1.1.3 Python Version and Core Dependencies

This book will assume readers are working with the following major dependencies and versions.

- Python 3.7+
- Pandas 1.0+
- Matplotlib 3.0+

I encourage readers to work within an Anaconda environment and use the `conda` package manager to take advantage of architecture-level optimizations that may outperform packages installed via `pip`.

1.2 GitHub Repo

The GitHub repo for this book can be found at https://github.com/chrisconlan/algorithmic-trading-with-python. Please download or clone the repo onto your machine in order to follow along with the code examples.

1.2.1 Repo Structure

- `src/` contains all of the code in the book laid out in a collections of scripts and modules.
- `listings/` contains all of the code snippets in the book laid out by order of appearance.
- `data/` contains all of the data we will use throughout the book, including 100 simulated assets and corresponding simulated alternative data sets.

1.2.2 Pull Requests and Issues Policy

I welcome all pull requests and issues on GitHub. Issues can be very general, ranging from broad discussions to specific bugs. Pull requests will only be accepted and merged into the repo if they fix a bug or represent a material improvement that does not fundamentally disagree with the layout of this book. If you would like to make extensions or modifications to the code that are not fundamental to the layout of this book, you are encouraged to fork the repo.

1.3 Source Data

We will be using simulated stock data throughout this book. The simulated data is stored in the GitHub repository, and the end-of-day (EOD) stock data itself is about 11MB. All of the stock tickers are fake, but we will refer to them as though they were real. See Section 2 of the preface to this book for a more thorough explanation of this decision.

Chapter 2

Performance Metrics

The fundamental goal of investing is to maximize risk-adjusted return. The fundamental goal of algorithmic trading is to develop a quantitative investing strategy that maximizes risk-adjusted return. In order to maximize it, we must be able to measure it. This chapter will introduce readers to various metrics that suit that purpose. In the process, we will discuss many standard definitions and practices in quantitative finance.

2.1 The Equity Curve

The equity curve is simply the evolution of the value of your portfolio over time. If you have an online stock brokerage, it might display a statistic called *equity*, *net liquidation value (NLV)*, or *account value* right when you log in. This usually represents the value of your cash holdings plus the value of your stock holdings.

Throughout this book, we will focus on the mathematics of unlevered long-only stock portfolios. The mathematics of portfolios using leverage, short positions, and/or derivatives are not only more complicated, but can be subject to opinionated changes according to the application domain.

2.1.1 Defining a Portfolio

For a single asset, we typically refer to a time series of prices as y_t for $t \in 0, ..., T$. When the asset is part of a collection of other assets, we refer to it as $y_{t,i}$ for asset $i \in I$, where I is the collection of all assets under consideration. Figure 2.1 shows the closing prices of AWU, BMG, and CUU, which can otherwise be referred to as $y_{t,i}$.

The portfolio value, P_t is simply the sum the collective holdings of the underlying assets at any given time. For example, if we say that a portfolio holds $w_{t,i}$ shares of asset i at time t, then the portfolio value can be expressed as the following.

$$P_t = \sum_{i \in I} w_{t,i} y_{t,i}$$

Figure 2.2 shows a sample portfolio where the account holds one third of a share of AWU, BMG, and CUU.

2.1.2 Defining the Equity Curve

The equity curve is the sum of cash holdings and stock holdings, less any transaction costs. So, for cash holdings defined as C_t, we have the following for the equity curve, E_t.

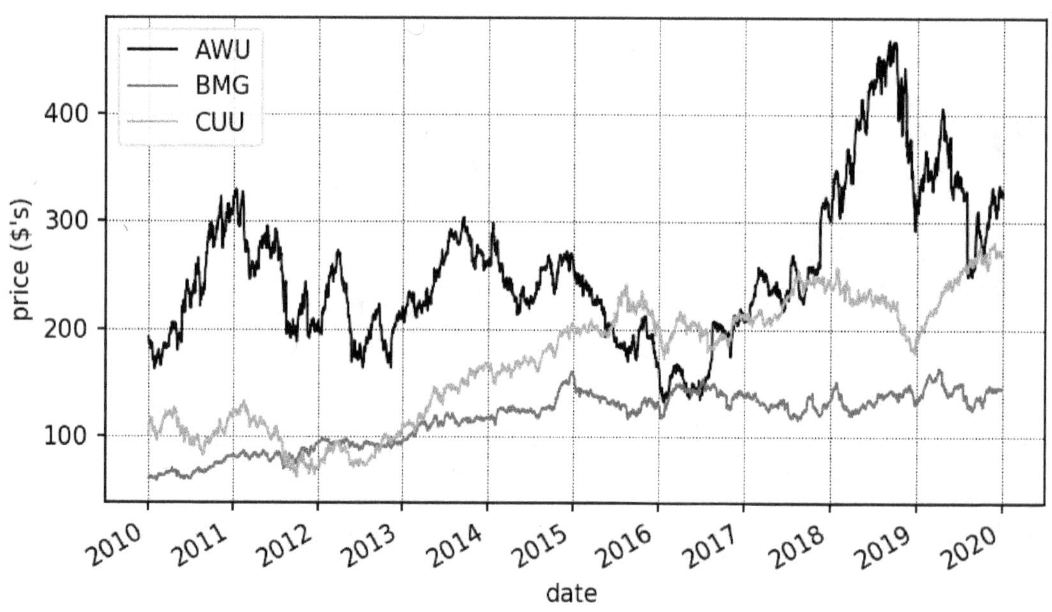

Figure 2.1: Sample closing prices $y_{t,i}$

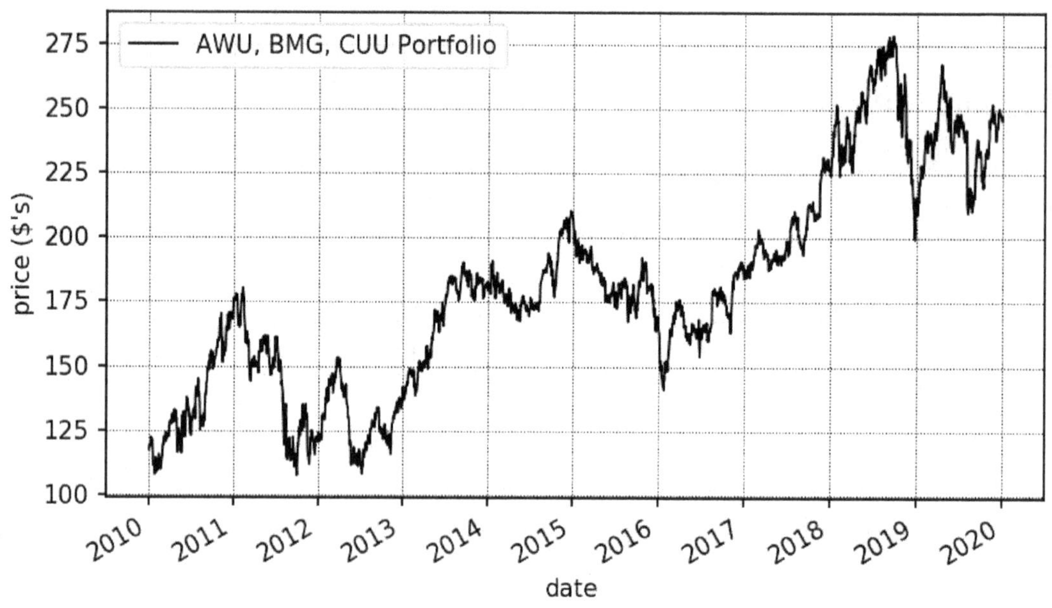

Figure 2.2: Sample portfolio

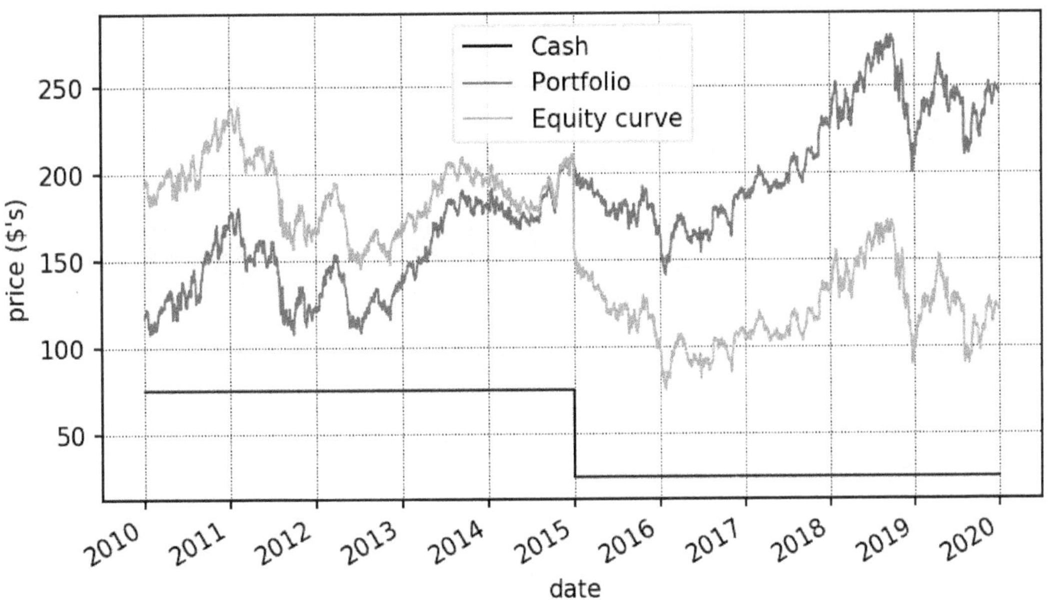

Figure 2.3: Sample equity curve

$$E_t = C_t + P_t$$

The equity of the account E_t is assumed to be measured after any trading and fee adjustments occur, against which the cash holdings and stock holdings can potentially change. In practice, fixed fees and percentage fees are reflected appropriately in C_t and P_t.

Figure 2.3 shows an equity curve constructed from the portfolio in Figure 2.2, where the cash holdings drop off from \$75 to \$25 halfway through, and the account occurs transaction costs of \$0.30 once every five days.

2.2 The Return Series

A return series is a series of price changes on the an asset, portfolio, or equity curve. Most typically, the return series refers to a series of percentage returns, but it might also refer to a series of dollar returns or logarithmic returns.

2.2.1 Percentage Returns

In the most simple case, the return on a stock series y_t can be represented as the following.

$$r_t = \frac{y_t - y_{t-1}}{y_{t-1}} = \frac{y_t}{y_{t-1}} - 1$$

Multiplying this result through by 100 will yield percentages that we commonly use in discussion. See Figure 2.4 for the return series of AWU.

Percentage returns have the following relationship with the price series, y_t.

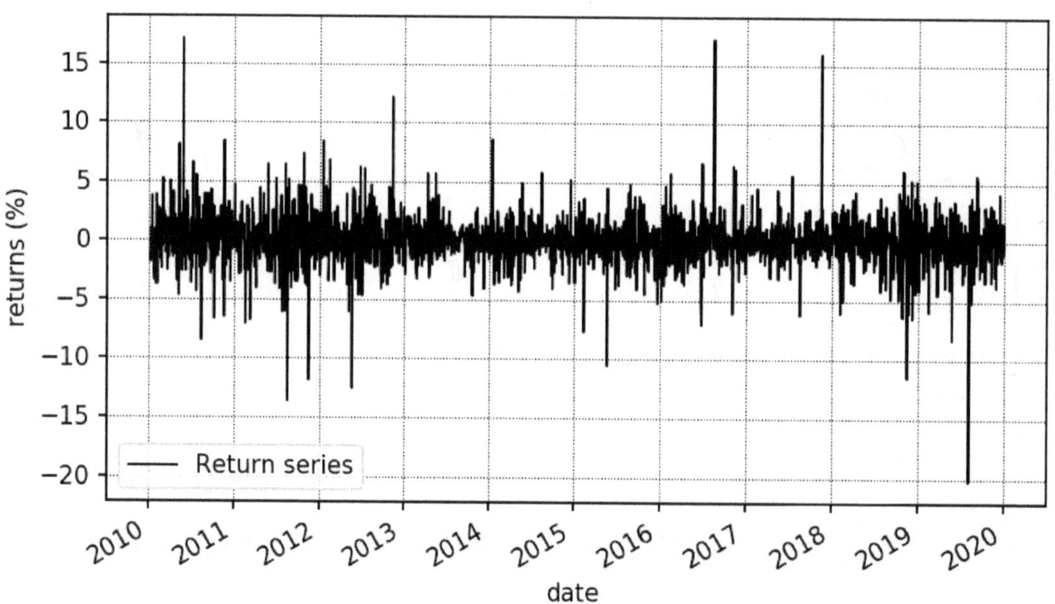

Figure 2.4: Sample return series

$$y_t = y_0 * \prod_{j=1}^{t}(1 + r_j)$$

Verbally, this means that any price y_t is the cumulative product of all of the intermediate returns from $0, ..., t$.

To calculate a return series in pure Python, you could do the following.

```
def calculate_return_series(prices: List[float]) -> List[float]:
    """
    Calculates return series as a parallel list of returns on prices
    """
    return_series = [None]
    for i in range(1, len(prices)):
        return_series.append((prices[i] / prices[i-1]) - 1)

    return return_series
```

Listing 2.1: Calculating the return series in pure Python

Note that we take care to output a list of values that is equal in length to the input list, and that r_0 is always undefined.

In practice we will calculate the return series in **pandas**, using the following code.

```
def calculate_return_series(series: pd.Series) -> pd.Series:
    """
    Calculates the return series of a time series.
    The first value will always be NaN.
    Output series retains the index of the input series.
    """
```

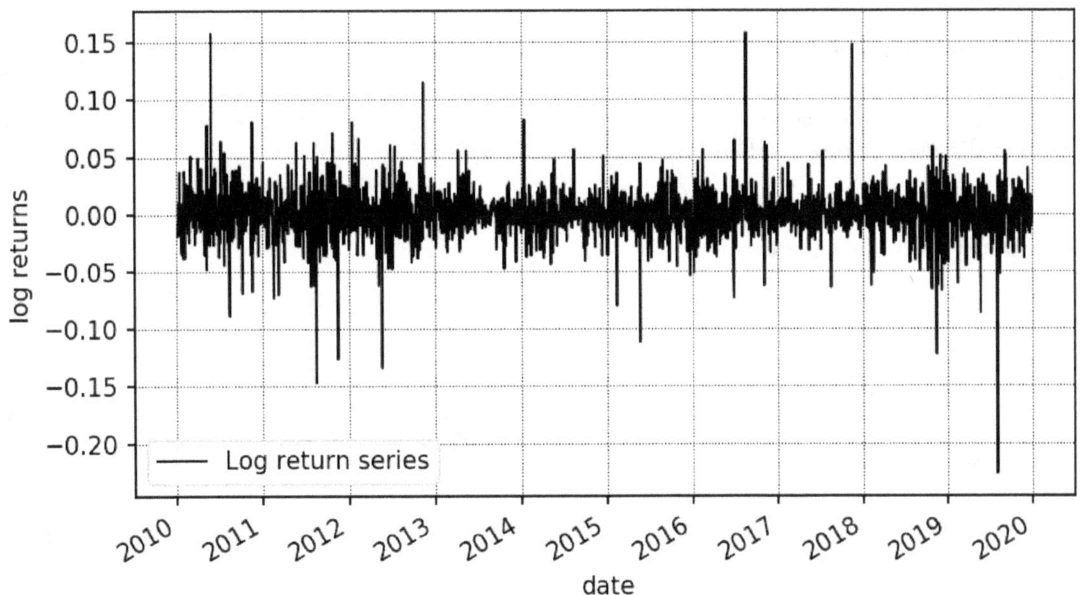

Figure 2.5: Sample log return series

```
    shifted_series = series.shift(1, axis=0)
    return series / shifted_series - 1
```

Listing 2.2: Calculating the return series with pandas

2.2.2 Log Returns

Log returns, which are commonly used to take advantage of their unique mathematical properties, can be represented as the following. See Figure 2.5 for the log return series of AWU.

$$r_t = \ln(\frac{y_t}{y_{t-1}}) = \ln y_t - \ln y_{t-1}$$

Log returns have the following relationship with the price series y_t.

$$y_t = y_0 * \exp[\sum_{j=1}^{t} r_j] = y_0 * \prod_{j=1}^{t} e^{r_j}$$

We can calculate the log return series in **pandas** with the following function.

```
def calculate_log_return_series(series: pd.Series) -> pd.Series:
    """
    Same as calculate_return_series but with log returns
    """
    shifted_series = series.shift(1, axis=0)
    return pd.Series(np.log(series / shifted_series))
```

Listing 2.3: Calculating the log return series with pandas

We will now move on to a discussion of the properties of each type of return series.

2.2.3 Properties of Return Series

The percentage return series and log return series have different properties and are used for different purposes. It is instructive to discuss those properties that might not be immediately obvious.

2.2.3.1 Symmetry and Interpretability

Percentage prices returns are not symmetrical, while log returns are. This point is best illustrated by example.

Imagine an unwieldy stock that loses 50% in value one day, then gains 50% in value the following day. Its percentage returns were -50% and +50%, respectively. If that stock started at $100 per share, it would have decreased to $50, then increased to $75. The percentage returns are symmetrical, but the price moves are not. This is because the true "reciprocal" of losing 50% in value is actually gaining 100% in value. In other words, if a stock loses half of its value, it must then double its value to return to its earlier price. On paper, $\frac{50}{100} - 1 = -0.5$ and $\frac{100}{50} - 1 = 1$.

This thinking extends to small price moves as well. To recoup a 1% loss, a stock must make a $\frac{100}{100-1} =$ 1.0101...% move upwards.

Log returns, on the other hand, are symmetrical. According to log returns, losing half of your value and doubling your value are truly reciprocal actions. On paper, $ln(50) - ln(100) \approx -0.693$ and $ln(100) - ln(50) \approx 0.693$.

As has been argued many times before, log returns are not easily interpretable for large price swings. It would not be very kind to share with your non-technical friends that your stock play made a 0.693 logarithmic return. As we will see, though, log returns are interpretable for small price swings, due to an interesting property.

2.2.3.2 Local Linearity

Elementary calculus makes the following interesting pair of assertions.

$$\frac{d}{dx}e^x = e^x$$

$$\frac{d}{dx}\ln x = \frac{1}{x}$$

This reveals another desirable property of log returns. The derivative of $\ln(x)$ near $x = 1$ is approximately 1. In other words, when $\ln(y_t/y_{t-1})$ is close to 1, which it nearly always is, a small increase or decrease in y_t will result in an nearly equal increase or decrease in r_t.

So, while we might not be able to guess the value of $\ln(300/100)$ in our heads, we can comfortably say $\ln(102/100) \approx 0.02$ or $\ln(99/100) \approx -0.01$. So, when discussing small fluctuations in stock prices with your non-technical peers, you can use logarithmic returns in secret and still be approximately factual.

Note that this only applies to the natural log, or log base-e. Other logarithms still exhibit local linearity, but not with a slope of 1.

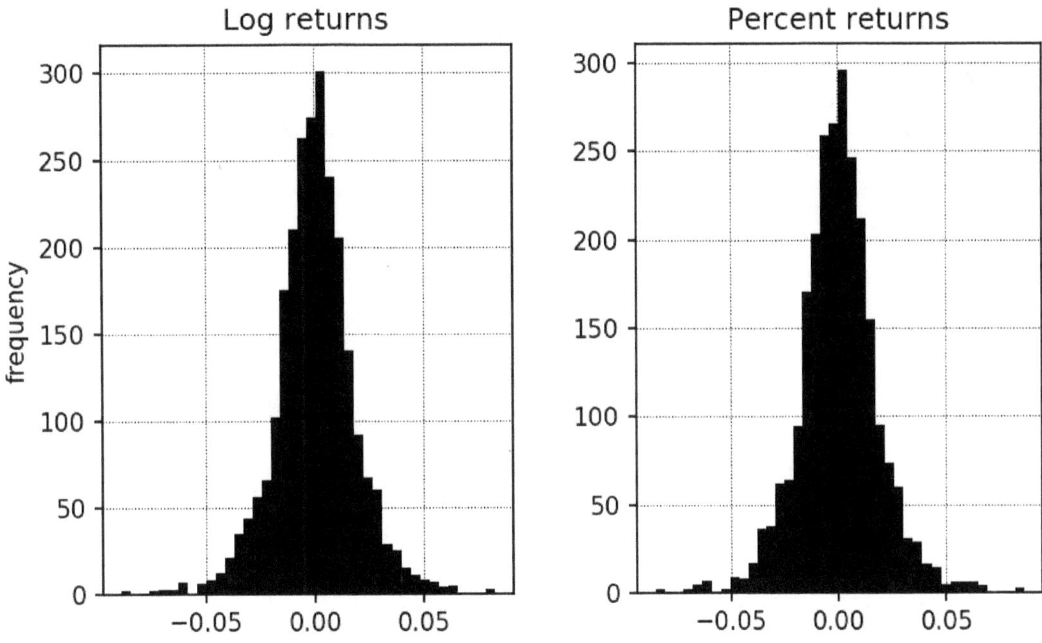

Figure 2.6: Log returns vs. percent returns

2.2.3.3 Tail Symmetry and Normality

Following from our discussion of symmetry, it is important to note that the ranges of percentage returns and log returns are different. Percentage returns have a range of $[-1, \infty]$ and log returns have a range of $[-\infty, \infty]$. In other words, while it is possible for a stock to go up 300% in value, it is not possible for it to go down 300% in value. It can only lose 100% of its value. Per log returns, losing 100% in value would correspond to $\ln(0/y_{t-1}) = -\infty$.

The issue of range becomes important when we start to think of returns as the outputs of statistical models. Many common statistical models assume that the error terms are normally distributed. Normal random variables are symmetric about their mean and have a range of $[-\infty, \infty]$. So, using log returns in this context is always more valid than using percentage returns. Though, in many cases, the underlying distributions of returns might not look that different from one another. See Figure 2.6 for a histogram of each type of return on AWU.

The return distribution of financial assets is a well-studied concept. The prevailing theory is that returns across most financial assets are log-normally distributed with fat tails. In other words, log returns exhibit normal distribution, but with more frequent extreme outcomes. This is consistent with the popular understanding of markets as exhibiting regular noise followed by occasional spikes and crashes.

2.3 Performance Metrics

Performance metrics allow us to evaluate strategies against one another and optimize variants of the same strategy. Most performance metrics are simple functions of the equity curve or return series. We will discuss some of them here.

2.3.1 Volatility

Before we begin discussing performance metrics, we need to discuss an important component that underlies many different metrics: volatility.

In finance, volatility generally refers to the sample standard deviation of a return series. While it would be nice if we could run `df['returns'].std()` and move on from this topic, there are some nuances to be discussed to ensure we can calculate volatility proficiently and express it conversationally.

To start, this is the statistical formula for measuring sample standard deviation. In statistics, the standard deviation refers to the *wideness* or *breadth* of a probability distribution for a random variable.

$$\sigma = \sqrt{\frac{\sum_{i=1}^{n}(x_i - \bar{x})^2}{n-1}}$$

Where $\bar{x}$ is the sample mean of the random variable, computed as follows.

$$\bar{x} = \frac{1}{n}\sum_{i=1}^{n} x_i$$

In finance, we typically measure the volatility of a return series via this formula, substituting r_i for x_i and T for n.

In finance, volatility is also assumed to be *annualized* if not otherwise stated. If we take the sample standard deviation σ_r for r_i, where r_i represents daily changes in prices of the underlying asset of portfolio, we obtain the *daily* volatility. To translate the daily volatility to the annualized volatility, we multiply σ_r by the square root of the number of trading days in the year. This is typically about 252 days.

I will spare readers the mathematical proof, but, the theory goes that, under the assumption that stock prices diffuse according to a log-normal Brownian motion, volatilities can be translated to different time intervals by multiplying through the square root of the difference. Quick experimentation shows this principle to be generally true.

For example, to obtain weekly volatility from daily volatility, multiply daily volatility by the square root of the number of trading days in a week, $\sqrt{5}$. To obtain yearly (or annualized) volatility from daily volatility, multiple daily volatility by $\sqrt{252}$. In practice, we can compute the adjustment factor of "5" or "252" on the fly based on the shape of the input data.

Further, in finance, volatility is assumed to calculated against log returns unless otherwise specified.

```
def get_years_past(series: pd.Series) -> float:
    """
    Calculate the years past according to the index of the series for use with
    functions that require annualization
    """
    start_date = series.index[0]
    end_date = series.index[-1]
    return (end_date - start_date).days / 365.25


def calculate_annualized_volatility(return_series: pd.Series) -> float:
    """
    Calculates annualized volatility for a date-indexed return series.
    Works for any interval of date-indexed prices and returns.
    """
    years_past = get_years_past(return_series)
```

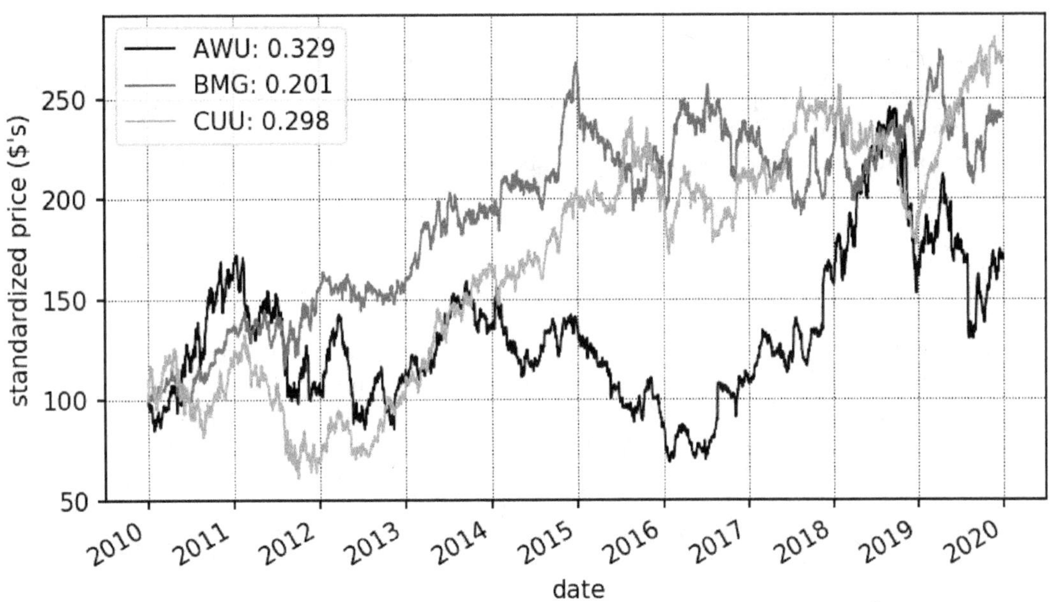

Figure 2.7: Volatility Comparison

```
    entries_per_year = return_series.shape[0] / years_past
    return return_series.std() * np.sqrt(entries_per_year)
```

Listing 2.4: Calculating annualized volatility

Applying this formula, we can see that the annualized volatility for AWU is about 33%. In other words, the standard deviation of yearly returns is estimated to be 33%. See Figure 2.7 for a comparison of annualized volatilities.

```
from pypm import data_io, metrics

df = data_io.load_eod_data('AWU')
return_series = metrics.calculate_log_return_series(df['close'])
print(metrics.calculate_annualized_volatility(return_series))
# Returns ...
# 0.3296226627596164
```

Listing 2.5: Calculating annualized volatility On AWU

We will apply these concepts to the calculation of various risk-adjusted return metrics.

2.3.2 Sharpe Ratio

The Sharpe Ratio is the most widely used and discussed performance metric because of its simplicity. In order to measure risk-adjusted return, we divide the return by a measure of risk. In this case, risk is an analogue to volatility as discussed above.

The formula for the Sharpe Ratio is as follows, where r_a is the annualized return on the portfolio, r_b is the annualized benchmark rate, and σ_r is the annualized volatility on percentage returns.

$$\frac{r_a - r_b}{\sigma_r}$$

Many texts offer too lean of an explanation of this concept, and the result has been the proliferation of unreliable and unstandardized Sharpe Ratios that can not be meaningfully compared to one another. In the past, I have recommended against its communication altogether. Here, I will attempt to give it a sufficiently detailed explanation, such that readers will be able to confidently discuss it in both a technical and conversational context.

2.3.2.1 CAGR

We have already discussed how to annualize volatility. Now, we will discuss how to annualize returns. The financial term for *annualized return* in this context is Compounded Annual Growth Rate, or CAGR. The CAGR answers the following question. Given a starting value, ending value, and length of time over which a portfolio evolves, what is the compounded annual rate of return that would achieve the same effect? The formula is as follows.

Note that the Sharpe Ratio can be calculated over an equity curve, portfolio, or single asset validly. In the following examples, we will use a single-asset portfolio of one share of AWU with no transaction costs called E_t.

$$r_a = CAGR = (\frac{E_T}{E_0})^{\frac{1}{k}} - 1$$

Where k represents the number of years spanned by T. As we did before with volatility, we can calculate k on the fly based on the dates in the `pd.Series` index. For daily returns, it will essentially be $\frac{T}{252}$.

```
def calculate_cagr(series: pd.Series) -> float:
    """
    Calculate compounded annual growth rate
    """
    value_factor = series.iloc[-1] / series.iloc[0]
    year_past = get_years_past(series)
    return (value_factor ** (1 / year_past)) - 1
```

Listing 2.6: Calculating CAGR

Applying this function, we can see that the CAGR on AWU over the 10 years for which we have data is about 5.5%. So, investing in AWU over ten years would be akin to receiving yearly compounded interest of 5.5% over ten years.

```
from pypm import data_io, metrics

df = data_io.load_eod_data('AWU')
print(metrics.calculate_cagr(df['close']))
# Returns ...
# 0.055545750640820346
```

Listing 2.7: Calculating CAGR on AWU

Up until this point in the book, I have included example code to implement some of the functions we have discussed, namely Listings 2.5 and 2.7. To avoid redundancy, we will refrain from doing so from now on unless the implementation is particularly illustrious.

Readers may notice that the CAGR itself is a performance metric. Optimizing a strategy for CAGR is akin to optimizing for overall returns, irrespective of risk.

2.3.2.2 The Benchmark Rate

I will say something that ought to be said. The benchmark rate is an opinion.

In the Sharpe Ratio formula, we define a value r_b that represents the annualized benchmark rate. The benchmark rate is an esoteric concept in finance and economics that is supposed to represent the risk-free rate of return from investing in U.S. government bonds. The thinking goes that, if your investment cash is not in the stock market (or some other high-risk asset), it is necessarily parked in something like a government bond that is accruing regular interest over time. In modern times, that is rarely the case. As of the time of writing, T-bill rates are at an all-time low. Further, checking and savings accounts do not accrue significant interest, and setting up a bond-investing account is a non-trivial activity. In my opinion, you are perfectly free to set the benchmark rate to zero in your calculations. If you would like to plug the 90-day T-bill annualized rate into your formulas, it is 1.1% as of March 1st, 2020.

We will assume a benchmark rate of zero throughout. When the benchmark rate is assumed to be zero, the Sharpe Ratio is sometime called High-Frequency Sharpe Ratio to reflect the relative insignificance of the benchmark returns over short time horizons.

2.3.2.3 Calculating the Sharpe Ratio

Putting all of the pieces together, we get the following formula for the Sharpe Ratio. Given that our single-share AWU portfolio had a 5.5% CAGR and 33% volatility, we have a Sharpe Ratio of 0.169.

```
def calculate_sharpe_ratio(price_series: pd.Series,
    benchmark_rate: float=0) -> float:
    """
    Calculates the sharpe ratio given a price series. Defaults to benchmark_rate
    of zero.
    """
    cagr = calculate_cagr(price_series)
    return_series = calculate_return_series(price_series)
    volatility = calculate_annualized_volatility(return_series)
    return (cagr - benchmark_rate) / volatility
```

Listing 2.8: Calculating Sharpe Ratio

See Figure 2.8 for a comparison of three stocks and their Sharpe Ratios. The starting prices of each stock are standardized to 100 to aid comparison. It is worth noting that CUU has a lower Sharpe Ratio than BMG despite returning more overall. This is evidence that CUU had higher volatility than BMG.

We will use many of the principles of the Sharpe Ratio to arrive at different performance metrics in the following sections.

2.3.3 Sortino Ratio

The Sortino Ratio is an attempt at an improvement on the Sharpe Ratio. Because the Sharpe Ratio uses vanilla volatility as its measure of risk, it penalizes both large upward and large downward price swings. The Sortino Ratio attempts to remedy this by only penalizing downward price swings. The formula is as follows.

$$\frac{r_a - r_b}{\sigma_d}$$

In this formulation, σ_d represents *downside deviation* of the return series, given the benchmark rate.

Earlier in this chapter, we presented the classical statistics formula for the standard deviation to illustrate how it is translated into finance to measure volatility. Instead of writing out code for this formula, we used

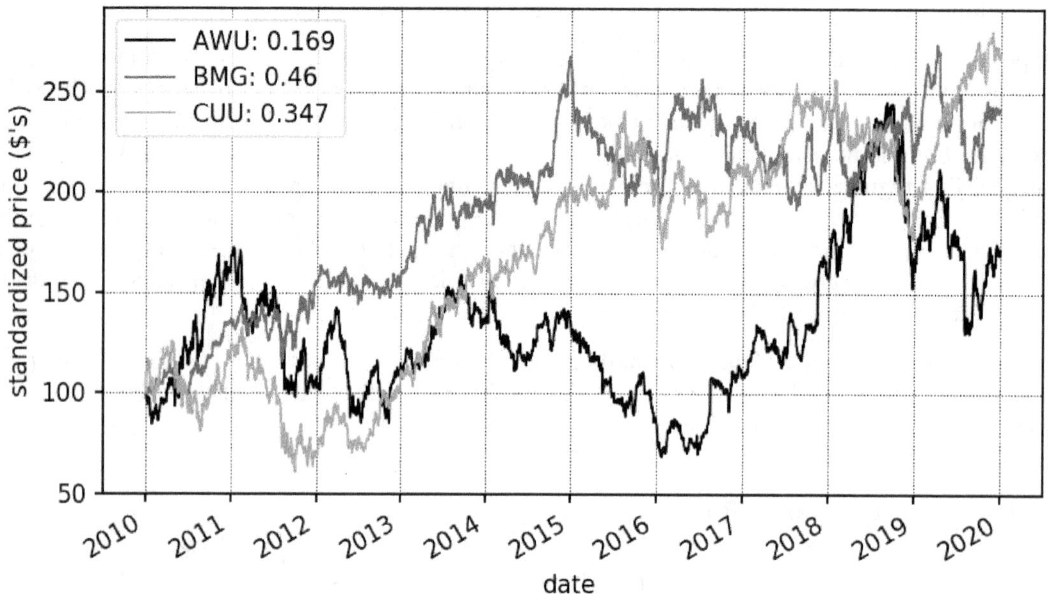

Figure 2.8: Sharpe Ratio Comparison

the built-in `pd.Series.std` function. The Sortino Ratio uses σ_d, for which there is no built-in function, so we will have to work through the code to compute it.

The formula for the downside volatility, the square of downside deviation, σ_d^2, is as follows.

$$\sigma_d^2 = \frac{1}{T-1} \sum_{t=1}^{T} \max\left[r_b - r_t, 0\right]^2$$

First, note the similarity to the equation for statistical standard deviation and for financial volatility. Instead of the sample mean return, $\bar{r}$, we use the benchmark rate r_b. Note how the inner term $r_b - r_t$ reflects the negative of the returns in excess of the benchmark rate. Further, the inner term $\max\left[r_b - r_t, 0\right]$ evaluates to zero whenever $r_t >= r_b$. Thus, positive returns in excess of the benchmark rate not counted towards volatility.

Just like with the Sharpe Ratio, we need to be careful about annualization and units of time throughout. The downside deviation needs to be annualized per the discussion in Section 2.3.1, but the benchmark rate also needs to be de-annualized when used in the downside deviation equation. In other words, in numerator of the Sortino Ratio, we want to compare the annualized portfolio return to the annualized benchmark return. In the denominator of the Sortino Ratio, we want to compare daily returns to the daily benchmark rate. Our code accounts for this, but other code may not. As mentioned previously, we will assume the benchmark rate is zero throughout our examples.

```
def calculate_annualized_downside_deviation(return_series: pd.Series,
    benchmark_rate: float=0) -> float:
    """
    Calculates the downside deviation for use in the sortino ratio.

    Benchmark rate is assumed to be annualized. It will be adjusted according
    to the number of periods per year seen in the data.
```

```
    """

    # For both de-annualizing the benchmark rate and annualizing result
    years_past = get_years_past(return_series)
    entries_per_year = return_series.shape[0] / years_past

    adjusted_benchmark_rate = ((1+benchmark_rate) ** (1/entries_per_year)) - 1

    downside_series = adjusted_benchmark_rate - return_series
    downside_sum_of_squares = (downside_series[downside_series > 0] ** 2).sum()
    denominator = return_series.shape[0] - 1
    downside_deviation = np.sqrt(downside_sum_of_squares / denominator)

    return downside_deviation * np.sqrt(entries_per_year)

def calculate_sortino_ratio(price_series: pd.Series,
    benchmark_rate: float=0) -> float:
    """
    Calculates the sortino ratio.
    """
    cagr = calculate_cagr(price_series)
    return_series = calculate_return_series(price_series)
    downside_deviation = calculate_annualized_downside_deviation(return_series)
    return (cagr - benchmark_rate) / downside_deviation
```

Listing 2.9: Calculating Sortino Ratio

Figures 2.9 and 2.10 show different values of the downside deviation and the Sortino Ratio for single-share portfolios of AWU, BMG, and CUU. For single-share portfolios, the Sortino Ratio and Sharpe Ratio evaluate performance very similarly. In more complex and well-diversified portfolios, the Sortino Ratio would reward managers more than the Sharpe Ratio for effectively reducing downside volatility.

2.3.4 Maximum Drawdown Statistics

The maximum drawdown is the maximum distance between the peak value of the equity curve and any value that follows the peak. In other words, it is the largest decline taken from a local maxima throughout the life of the portfolio.

The maximum drawdown is a more parametric measure of performance than those previously discussed. By parametric, I mean that it does not rely so much on the underpinnings of classical statistics. There are a few versions of max drawdown statistics that are worth discussing.

2.3.4.1 The Max Drawdown and Drawdown Series

The drawdown series is a time series representing drawdown from the rolling maximum at every time, t. The maximum of the drawdown series is the maximum drawdown.

```
from typing import Dict, Any, Callable

DRAWDOWN_EVALUATORS: Dict[str, Callable] = {
    'dollar': lambda price, peak: peak - price,
    'percent': lambda price, peak: -((price / peak) - 1),
    'log': lambda price, peak: np.log(peak) - np.log(price),
}
```

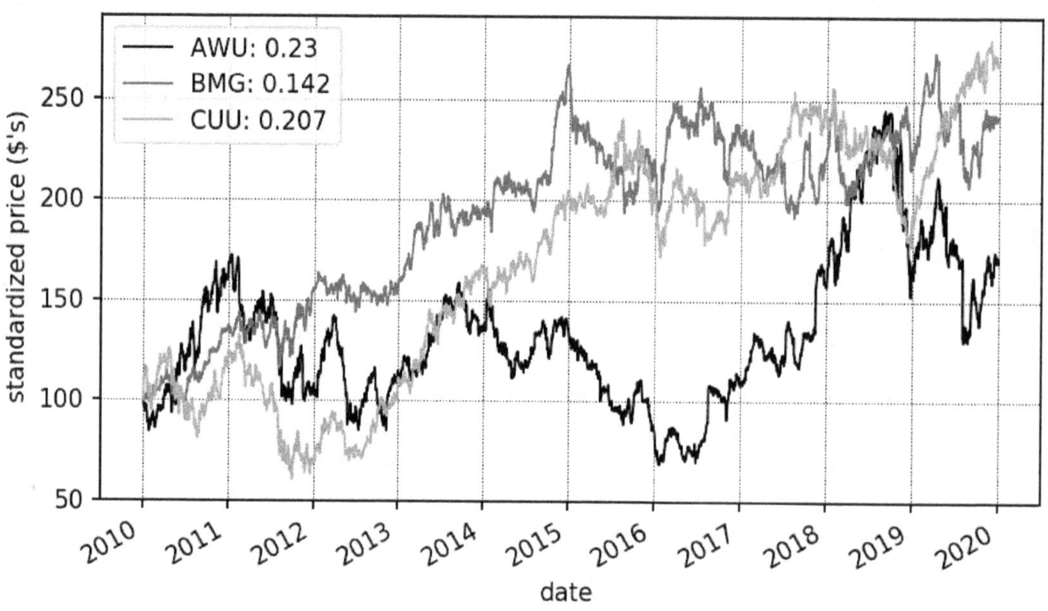

Figure 2.9: Downside Deviation Comparison

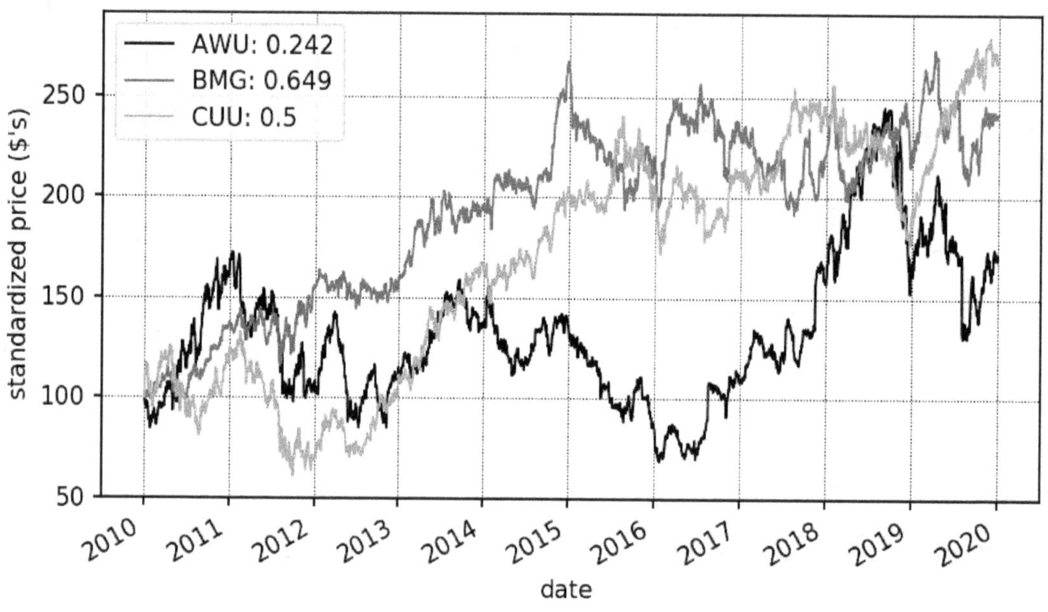

Figure 2.10: Sortino Ratio Comparison

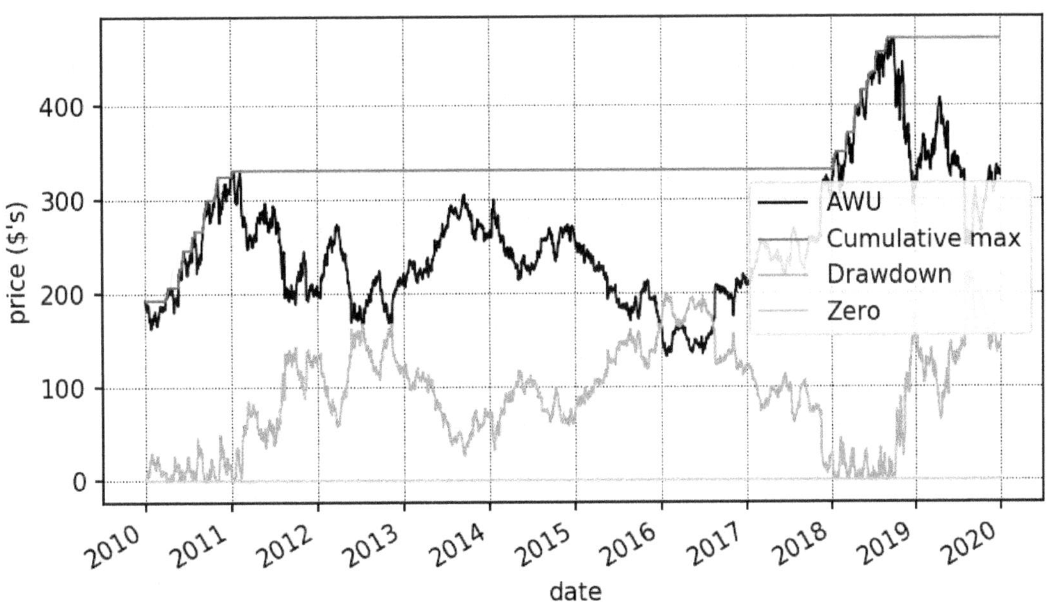

Figure 2.11: Drawdown Series Sample

```
def calculate_drawdown_series(series: pd.Series, method: str='log') -> pd.Series:
    """
    Returns the drawdown series
    """
    assert method in DRAWDOWN_EVALUATORS, \
        f'Method "{method}" must by one of {list(DRAWDOWN_EVALUATORS.keys())}'

    evaluator = DRAWDOWN_EVALUATORS[method]
    return evaluator(series, series.cummax())

def calculate_max_drawdown(series: pd.Series, method: str='log') -> float:
    """
    Simply returns the max drawdown as a float
    """
    return calculate_drawdown_series(series, method).max()
```

Listing 2.10: Computing maximum drawdown

See Figure 2.11 for a visual example of the drawdown series on AWU for `method='dollar'`.

It is often useful to know the date and price of the peak and trough when analyzing the maximum drawdown. The following function returns the max drawdown with such metadata.

```
def calculate_max_drawdown_with_metadata(series: pd.Series,
    method: str='log') -> Dict[str, Any]:
    """
    Calculates max_drawdown and stores metadata about when and where. Returns
    a dictionary of the form
        {
```

```
            'max_drawdown': float,
            'peak_date': pd.Timestamp,
            'peak_price': float,
            'trough_date': pd.Timestamp,
            'trough_price': float,
        }
    """

    assert method in DRAWDOWN_EVALUATORS, \
        f'Method "{method}" must by one of {list(DRAWDOWN_EVALUATORS.keys())}'

    evaluator = DRAWDOWN_EVALUATORS[method]

    max_drawdown = 0
    local_peak_date = peak_date = trough_date = series.index[0]
    local_peak_price = peak_price = trough_price = series.iloc[0]

    for date, price in series.iteritems():

        # Keep track of the rolling max
        if price > local_peak_price:
            local_peak_date = date
            local_peak_price = price

        # Compute the drawdown
        drawdown = evaluator(price, local_peak_price)

        # Store new max drawdown values
        if drawdown > max_drawdown:
            max_drawdown = drawdown

            peak_date = local_peak_date
            peak_price = local_peak_price

            trough_date = date
            trough_price = price

    return {
        'max_drawdown': max_drawdown,
        'peak_date': peak_date,
        'peak_price': peak_price,
        'trough_date': trough_date,
        'trough_price': trough_price
    }
```

Listing 2.11: Computing maximum drawdown metadata

This metadata allows us to plot the path of the drawdown. Figure 2.12 shows the path of the dollar and percentage max drawdowns on AWU. The log max drawdown will always have the same path as the percentage max drawdown, so it is not shown here. The log max drawdown for this example is 0.918.

Figure 2.12: Drawdown Paths Sample

2.3.4.2 Log Max Drawdown Ratio

The log max drawdown ratio divides the log return on the overall portfolio by the log max drawdown. Like the Sharpe Ratio, it uses a measure of profitability in the numerator and measure of risk in the denominator.

The formula is as follows, where y_p and y_q are the prices at the peak and trough of the drawdown path, respectively.

$$MD_{log} = (\ln y_T - \ln y_0) - (\ln y_p - \ln y_q)$$

The code to compute this is simple, following from our discussion of calculating the max drawdown.

```
def calculate_log_max_drawdown_ratio(series: pd.Series) -> float:
    log_drawdown = calculate_max_drawdown(series, method='log')
    log_return = np.log(series.iloc[-1]) - np.log(series.iloc[0])
    return log_return - log_drawdown
```

Listing 2.12: Computing log max drawdown ratio

It is worth noting that the log max drawdown ratio is neither parametric nor annualized. As a standalone number, it gives a relative idea of how much more significant the return was than the max drawdown.

2.3.4.3 Calmar Ratio

The Calmar Ratio is worth mentioning because it is one of the most common risk-return metrics that makes use of the maximum drawdown. The Calmar Ratio can be verbally defined as the percentage max drawdown ratio computed over a three year trailing period.

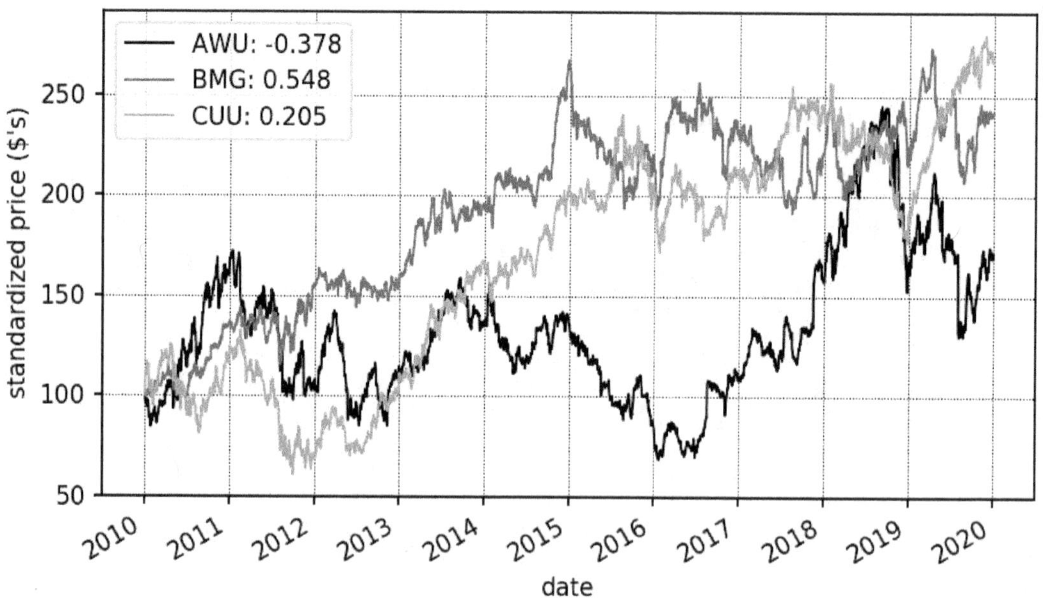

Figure 2.13: Log Max Drawdown Ratios

It is best to just explain this one via our existing code. In the following chart, we computed the Calmar Ratio over a 10 year period to allow easier comparison against our other metrics.

```
def calculate_calmar_ratio(series: pd.Series, years_past: int=3) -> float:
    """
    Return the percent max drawdown ratio over the past three years using
    CAGR as the numerator, otherwise known as the Calmar Ratio
    """

    # Filter series on past three years
    last_date = series.index[-1]
    three_years_ago = last_date - pd.Timedelta(days=years_past*365.25)
    series = series[series.index > three_years_ago]

    # Compute annualized percent max drawdown ratio
    percent_drawdown = calculate_max_drawdown(series, method='percent')
    cagr = calculate_cagr(series)
    return cagr / percent_drawdown
```

Listing 2.13: Computing Calmar Ratio

2.3.5 Regression-based Statistics

Regression-based statistics use linear regression in one way or another to evaluate investment performance. We will give an example of one that measures the linearity of the equity curve, and another that regresses portfolio returns against benchmark returns.

The equation for a simple linear regression is as follows.

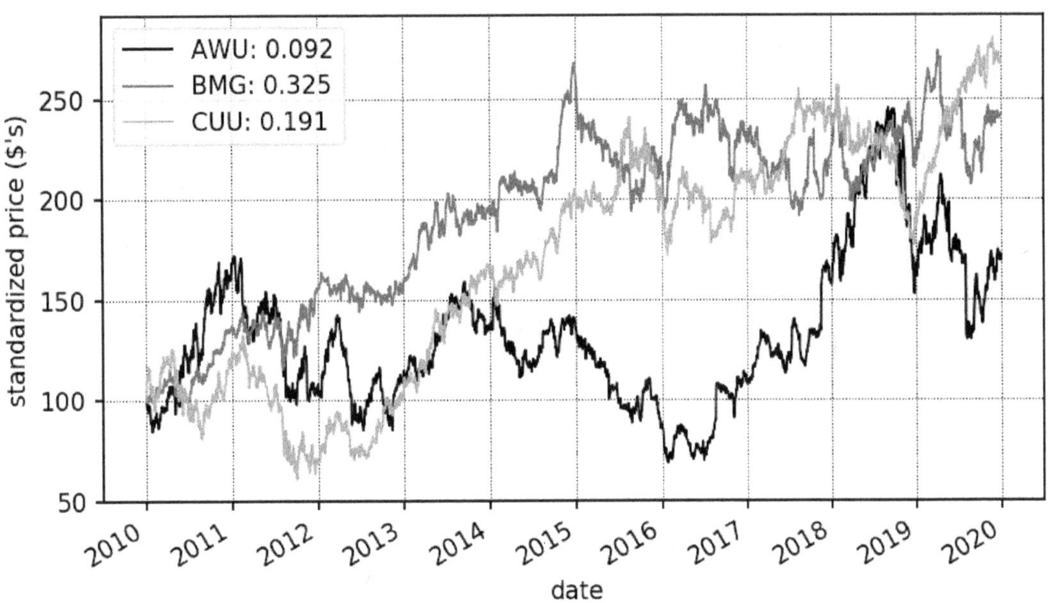

Figure 2.14: 10-year Calmar Ratios

$$y_i = \alpha + \beta x_i + \epsilon_i$$

The best-fitting line is achieved when the sum of squared errors, $SSE = \sum_{i=1}^{n} \epsilon_i^2$ is minimized. In the above formulation, α represents the y-intercept of the best fitting line on a scatter plot of x_i against y_i. Similarly, β represents the slope of the line.

The r-squared value, R^2, of the regression represents the proportion of variance between X and Y accounted for by the linear regression. It is bounded between 0 and 1. As an aside, the $\sqrt{R^2} = R$ is the magnitude of the correlation between X and Y, regardless of the existence of a regression.

The following performance metrics will use various aspects of this equation to attempt to arrive at a robust measure of risk-adjusted return.

2.3.5.1 Pure Profit Score (PPS)

The Pure Profit Score scales the annualized portfolio return against the linearity of the equity curve.

$$PPS = r_a * R^2$$

In the above formulation, R^2 is the r-squared of the following regression of the equity curve against time.

$$E_t = \alpha + \beta t + \epsilon_t$$

The motivation behind this performance metric is very simple. If the equity curve is a straight line, indicating consistent daily profit, the R^2 will be 1, and thus will not penalize the annualized return.

Figure 2.15: Pure Profit Score on AWU

Computing this score in Python is easy with the aid of `scikit-learn`. See the following figures for examples of the PPS and regression line on AWU and BMG.

```
from sklearn.linear_model import LinearRegression

def calculate_pure_profit_score(price_series: pd.Series) -> float:
    """
    Calculates the pure profit score
    """
    cagr = calculate_cagr(price_series)

    # Build a single column for a predictor, t
    t: np.ndarray = np.arange(0, price_series.shape[0]).reshape(-1, 1)

    # Fit the regression
    regression = LinearRegression().fit(t, price_series)

    # Get the r-squared value
    r_squared = regression.score(t, price_series)

    return cagr * r_squared
```

Listing 2.14: Computing Pure Profit Score

2.3.5.2 Jensen's Alpha

Jensen's Alpha is the α of the following regression.

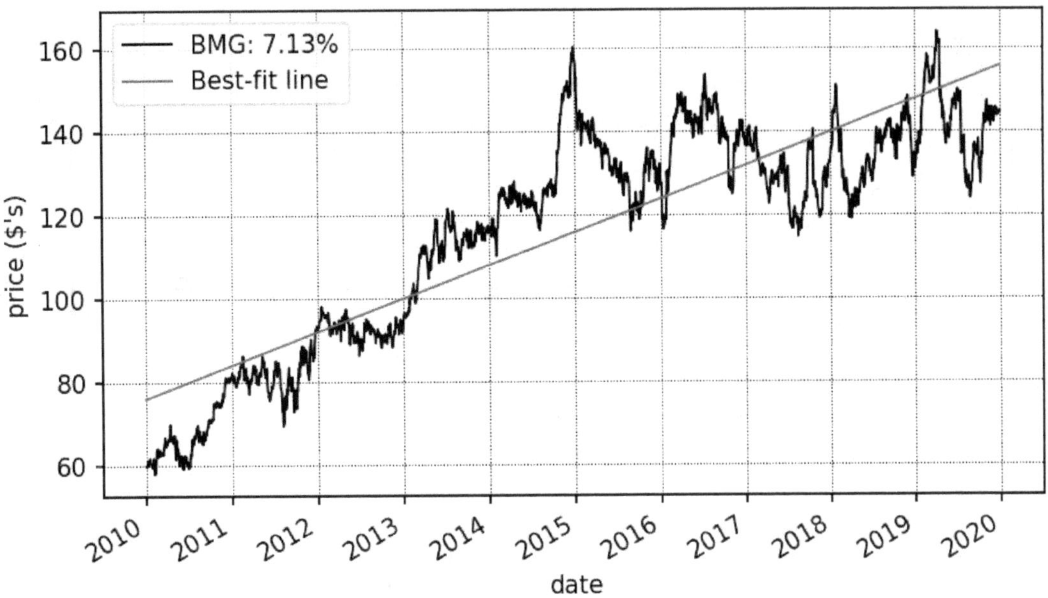

Figure 2.16: Pure Profit Score on BMG

$$r_t = \alpha + \beta q_t + \epsilon_t$$

In the above formulation, q_t represents the return series on a benchmark index at time t, and r_t represents the return series for the equity curve under consideration.

Jensen's Alpha was originally developed to attempt to measure the performance of mutual funds against the overall market. The idea is as follows. If a mutual fund returns more than the overall market on a good day, and loses less than the overall market on a bad day, the value of α will be positive. This behavior would represent intelligent and active management that surpasses passive investing strategies, and would yield a positive Jensen's Alpha. Alternatively, if a mutual fund returns more on good days and loses more on bad days, the fund is simply simulating the effect of financial leverage. This does not reflect intelligent and active management, and would yield a Jensen's Alpha of zero.

As mentioned previously, many popular statistical models assume that the error terms are normally distributed. Linear regression is one of those models. Therefore, we will use log returns when calculating Jensen's Alpha. See Section 2.2 on return series for a more thorough explanation.

See Figure 2.17 for a simulated portfolio that has a positive Jensen's Alpha. It is worth noting that most individual stocks have a significant enough correlation with the overall market that their Jensen's Alpha is statistically zero when treating the stock as a single-asset portfolio.

Statistics-savvy readers may notice that it is possible to calculate confidence bounds on the Jensen's Alpha that can be used for statistical inference. We will refrain from exploring this because it is not immediately useful in the context of portfolio optimization. Additionally, `sklearn` does not natively support confidence bounds on parameters of its models. Those interested are encouraged to check out the `patsy` and `statsmodels` libraries.

```
def calculate_jensens_alpha(return_series: pd.Series,
    benchmark_return_series: pd.Series) -> float:
```

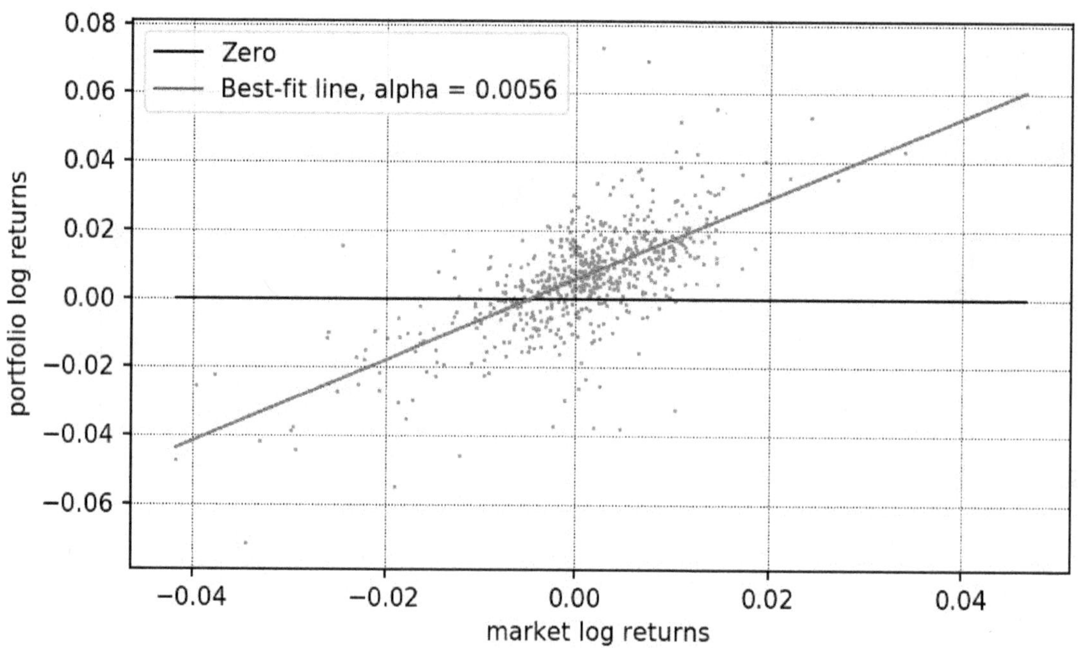

Figure 2.17: Jensen's Alpha on Simulated Portfolio

```
"""
Calculates jensens alpha. Prefers input series have the same index. Handles
NAs.
"""

# Join series along date index and purge NAs
df = pd.concat([return_series, benchmark_return_series], sort=True, axis=1)
df = df.dropna()

# Get the appropriate data structure for scikit learn
clean_returns: pd.Series = df[return_series.name]
clean_benchmarks = pd.DataFrame(df[benchmark_return_series.name])

# Fit a linear regression and return the alpha
regression = LinearRegression().fit(clean_benchmarks, y=clean_returns)
return regression.intercept_
```

Listing 2.15: Calculating Jensen's Alpha

Jensen's Alpha has had a significant cultural impact on finance. When traders conversationally refer to *alpha* and *beta* when discussing strategies and portfolios, they are typically referring to those values as defined in this regression. Even among traders that do not necessarily appreciate the underlying mathematics, the term *high alpha* is used conversationally to denote strategies that beat the market on this basis. The popular financial blogging website Seeking Alpha follows the same etymology.

2.4 Conclusion

In this chapter, we defined numerous metrics for risk-adjusted return and explored key concepts and standards of computational finance in the process. In the next chapter, we will explore technical indicators.

In portfolio optimization, technical indicators function as signals, and risk-return metrics function as objective variables. In later chapters, we will discuss how to adjust the way we generate signals in order to maximize an objective variable.

Chapter 3

Technical Indicators

Technical indicators are functions of the market activity for a financial asset. They attempt to uncover patterns in market behavior using market activity data to produce trading signals. Readers are probably familiar with common technical indicators like the simple moving average, which is a rolling average of the price history.

This chapter will serve as a light introduction to technical indicators. In practice, technical indicators are only useful insofar as we can use them to produce statistically significant returns. In the following chapters, we will apply what we learned here to determine if these technical indicators can do so.

3.1 Rolling Functions and Algorithms

Technical indicators will generally be rolling functions that return a data structure equal in shape to the input. A rolling computation will have some type of *window* over which some computations is performed. For example, a simple trailing window of length m will supply entries entries of y_i from $t - m - 1$ through t at time t to some function. More complex windows like triangular or Gaussian windows will provide a section of data and a weight for each data point.

3.1.1 Simple Moving Average

The most simple yet relevant example in financial analysis is the simple moving average (SMA). The simple moving average for m periods is simply the average of the past m data points. The formula is as follows. Throughout this chapter we will use z_t to refer to the values of various indicators. See Figure 3.1 for simple moving averages with $m = 5$ and $m = 34$ on AWU.

$$z_t = \frac{1}{m} \sum_{i=0}^{m-1} y_{t-i}$$

The code for this is strikingly simple with **pandas**.

```
def calculate_simple_moving_average(series: pd.Series, n: int=20) -> pd.Series:
    """Calculates the simple moving average"""
    return series.rolling(n).mean()
```

Listing 3.1: Calculating the simple moving average in pandas

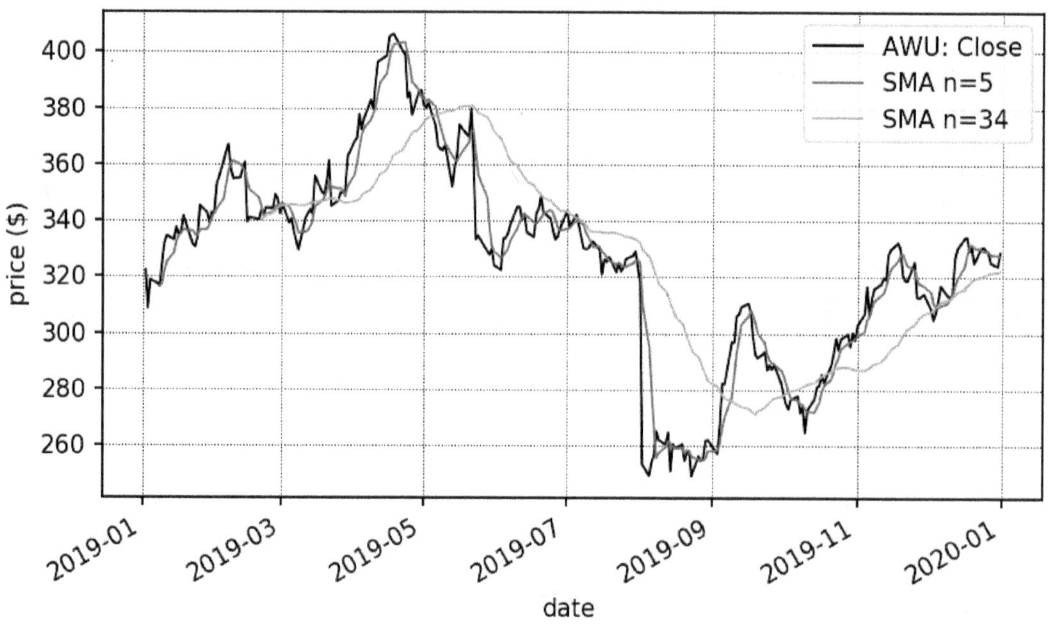

Figure 3.1: Simple Moving Averages on AWU

The **pandas** package provides us with an interface to rolling windows via the `.rolling(n)` method for both `pd.DataFrame` and `pd.Series` objects. From here, we can access a number of built-in **pandas** functions like `.sum()`, `.mean()`, `.min()`, and `.max()`, even `.std()`. There is a lot going on under the hood here, so we will break down what is going on in pure Python. Not all of the rolling calculations we do on **pandas** objects will be clean and simple like this, so it is instructive to understand how to write efficient rolling functions in pure Python.

3.1.2 Efficient Windowing Functions

This section will assume readers have a basic understanding of computational complexity and Big-Oh notation. Readers that are not familiar with these concepts are encouraged to read Appendix A for an introduction.

The point of this section is very simple: It is very easy to accidentally write inefficient code when dealing with windowing functions. Most windowing functions can be optimized to run in $O(n)$ time for a series of length n. When dealing with a window of length m, it is very common to see code that needlessly runs in $O(nm)$ time. I have seen seasoned professionals do so accidentally, and I have done so myself. I have even published such accidents in previous works of mine, even going so far as to parallelize them to increase computation speed.

The following listing shows an inefficient calculation of a simple moving average in pure Python.

```
def slow_moving_average(values: List[float], m: int=20):
    """
    This is O(nm) time, because it re-computes the sum at every step
    1 + 2 + 3 + 4 + ... / m
    2 + 3 + 4 + 5 + ... / m
    3 + 4 + 5 + 6 + ... / m
    4 + 5 + 6 + 7 + ... / m
```

```
    and so on ...
    Leading to approx (m-1) * n individual additions.
    """

    # Initial values
    moving_average = [None] * (m-1)

    for i in range(m-1, len(values)):
        the_average = np.mean(values[(i-m+1):i+1])
        moving_average.append(the_average)

    return moving_average
```

Listing 3.2: Calculating the simple moving average inefficiently

The above algorithm is taking the mean of a section of a list of length m for each iteration of the loop. This is a dead giveaway that it is behaving inefficiently. We do not need to completely recalculate the mean each time. We can drop the last element of the intermediate sum, then add in the current element before taking the average.

See Figures 3.2 and 3.3 for an execution time profile of these functions. The slow moving average computes in $O(nm)$ time, while the fast moving average and **pandas** moving average compute in $O(n)$ time.

```
def fast_moving_average(values: List[float], m: int=20):
    """
    This is O(n) time, because it keeps track of the intermediate sum.
    Leading to approx 2n individual additions.
    """

    # Initial values
    moving_average = [None] * (m-1)
    accumulator = sum(values[:m])
    moving_average.append(accumulator / m)

    for i in range(m, len(values)):
        accumulator -= values[i-m]
        accumulator += values[i]
        moving_average.append(accumulator / m)

    return moving_average
```

Listing 3.3: Calculating the simple moving average efficiently

The **pandas** moving average outperforms both functions by a huge margin for large inputs because it takes advantage of compiled code made specifically for this purpose. The reason otherwise efficient algorithms run faster in **pandas** and **numpy** than in pure Python is known as *vectorization*. We will proceed under the assumption that native **pandas** functions are preferred to pure Python algorithms, and all algorithms ought to be computationally efficient.

There is no one-size-fits-all solution for avoiding inefficient rolling functions. Bringing any algorithm from a state of inefficiency to a state of efficiency will require creative application of domain knowledge to reuse values from previous windows in current windows, as we did with the simple moving average above.

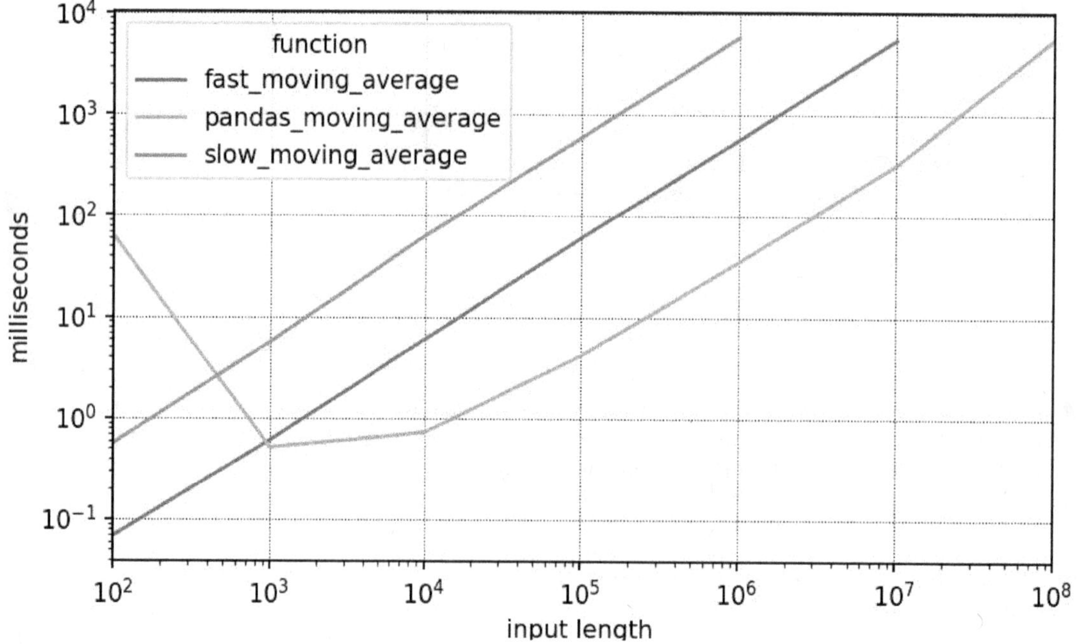

Figure 3.2: Computation time for various SMA functions

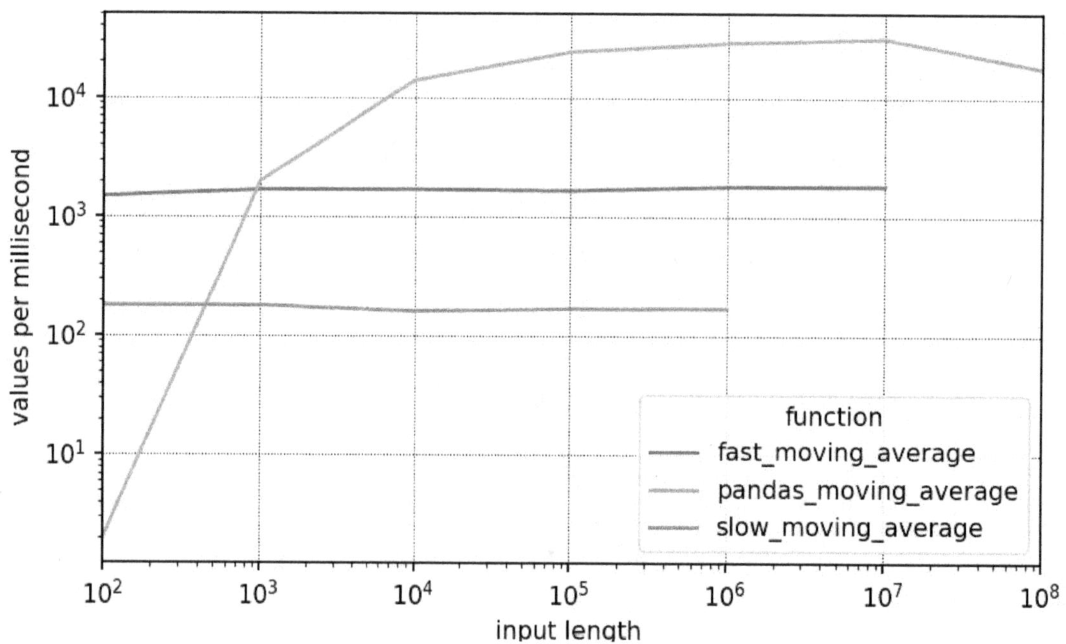

Figure 3.3: Values processed per millisecond for various SMA functions

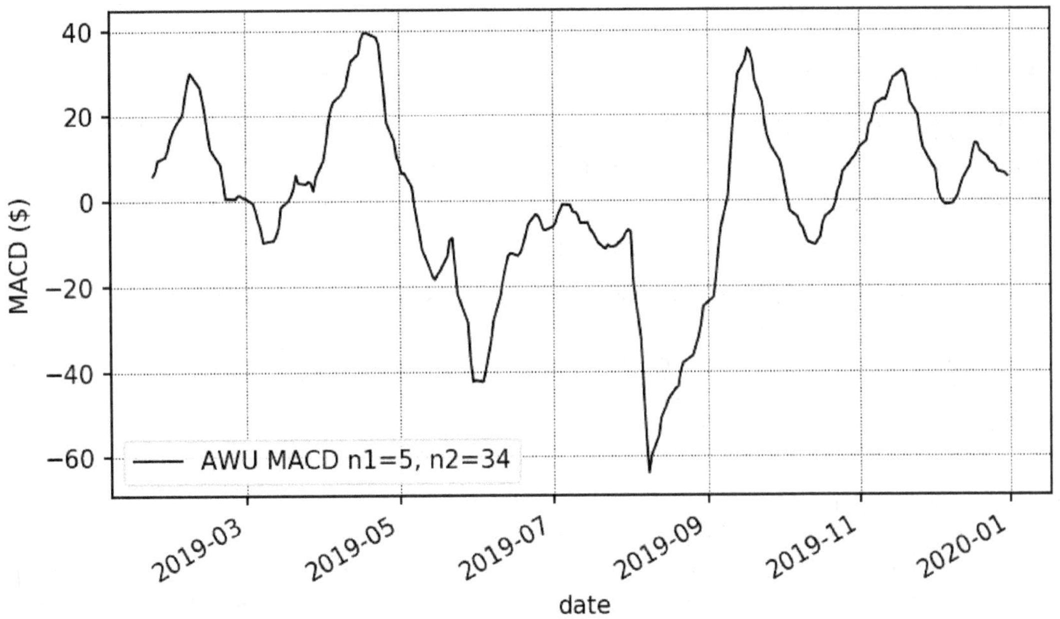

Figure 3.4: MACD on AWU

3.2 Oscillators

The first major class of indicators we will discuss are called oscillators. Oscillators commonly have a relationship to the first derivative of an asset's underlying price history, and often appear under the price history in financial charting software. In other words, these indicators appear under the price history chart, on a different chart, because they do not share a vertical axis with the price history. Further, they are classified as oscillators because they tend to either revert to zero or ping-pong between a maximum and minimum. As we will see, this tendency is mathematically intrinsic.

Popular oscillators include the Moving Average Convergence Divergence Oscillator (MACD) and the Relative Strength Index (RSI).

3.2.1 Moving Average Convergence Divergence Oscillator (MACD)

The MACD oscillator is the difference between two moving averages of different lengths. As the name implies, the moving averages tend converge and diverge regularly, so long as the stock does not march forward in a perfectly straight line. Thus, the difference appears to oscillate, unbounded, between negative and positive values.

The expanded formula is as follows, for a short moving average with length n_1 and a long moving average with length n_2.

$$z_t = \frac{1}{n_1} \sum_{i=0}^{n_1 - 1} y_{t-i} - \frac{1}{n_2} \sum_{i=0}^{n_2 - 1} y_{t-i}$$

See Figure 3.4 for an example of a MACD calculated on AWU. Readers may notice that the MACD here is the difference between the two moving averages plotted on Figure 3.1.

```
def calculate_macd_oscillator(series: pd.Series,
    n1: int=5, n2: int=34) -> pd.Series:
    """
    Calculate the moving average convergence divergence oscillator, given a
    short moving average of length n1 and a long moving average of length n2
    """
    assert n1 < n2, f'n1 must be less than n2'
    return calculate_simple_moving_average(series, n1) - \
        calculate_simple_moving_average(series, n2)
```

Listing 3.4: Calculating the MACD Oscillator

The indicators we will discuss in this chapter were formulated theoretically by technical analysts who sought to use them to generate trading signals to make profits in the market. Some of the indicators we discuss may seem a little contrived or may have been conceived on flimsy evidence. Nonetheless, we will discuss how those technical analysts used these indicators to generate signals. It will be up to us, using simulation methods we discuss later, to determine if those trading signals and indicators provide any value to investors.

The MACD indicator is traditionally used as a momentum-based entry signal. A buy signal occurs when the MACD line crosses from below zero to above zero. A sell signal occurs when the MACD line crosses from above zero to below zero. It is a momentum-based indicator in the sense that, in order for it to cross the zero-line, there has to have been some short-term directional momentum in the asset price. So, when traders use the MACD to enter trades, they are attempting to "follow" the directional momentum of the price.

The opposite of a momentum-based indicator is a reversal-based indicator. We will touch on this later in the chapter, after discussing a few more indicators.

3.3 Overlays

The second major class of indicators we will discuss are called overlays. Overlays are generally related to the stock price in both units and position, and the information we get from overlays has to do with the relationship between the overlay and the stock price itself. The indicators typically appear on the same chart as the price history, or *overlayed* on the price history.

Popular indicators include the Bollinger Bands and the Ichimoku Cloud.

3.3.1 Bollinger Bands

The Bollinger Bands combine moving averages with an alternative measure of volatility to create a 3 part overlay. The Bollinger Bands consist of three bands: an upper, middle, and lower band. The middle band is typically a 20-day simple moving average, and the other bands are the middle bands plus and minus a 20-day rolling standard deviation of the prices. We will forgo a mathematical formula and explain this via code.

```
def calculate_bollinger_bands(series: pd.Series, n: int=20) -> pd.DataFrame:
    """
    Calculates the bollinger bands and returns them as a dataframe
    """

    sma = calculate_simple_moving_average(series, n)
    stdev = calculate_simple_moving_sample_stdev(series, n)

    return pd.DataFrame({
        'middle': sma,
```

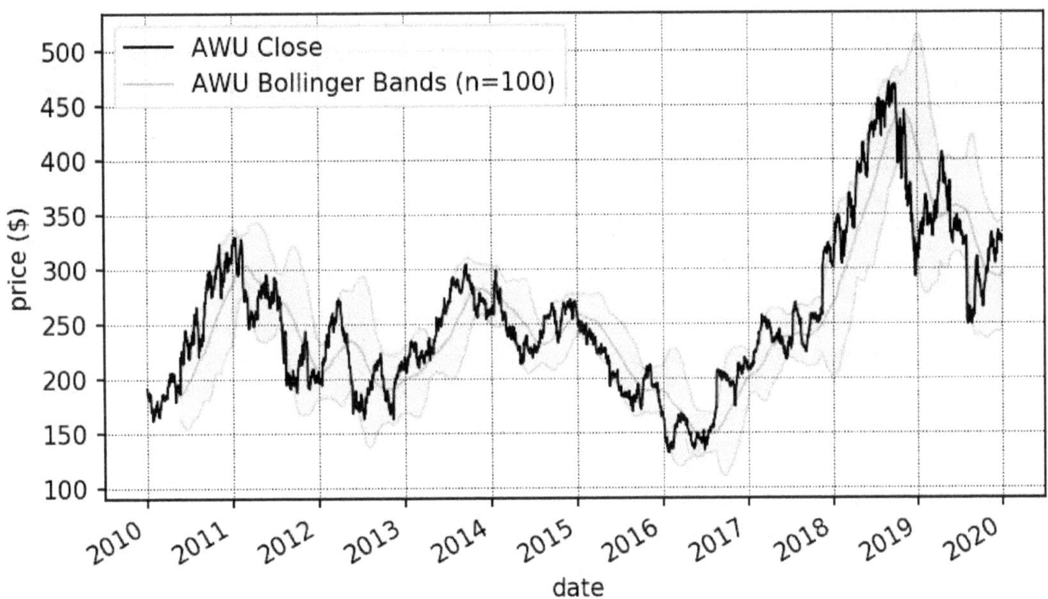

Figure 3.5: Bollinger Bands on AWU

```
        'upper': sma + 2 * stdev,
        'lower': sma - 2 * stdev
})
```

Listing 3.5 Calculate Bollinger Bands

Note that the standard deviation is not taken against the return series, as is typical when discussing volatility. It is taken against the price series, which, in itself, only has statistical relevance when done over very short periods.

See Figure 3.5 for an example of the Bollinger Bands overlaid on AWU. We have in-painted the area between the upper and lower bands to more easily indicate when price series is outside of the bands.

There is some controversy regarding how the Bollinger Bands should be used to generate trading signals. Nonetheless, I believe the price moving outside of the bands constitutes a perfectly valid reversal signal. In other words, the price crossing above the upper band indicates a sell signal, and the price crossing below the lower band indicates a buy signal. This is a reversal signal in the sense that the price has to move considerably in the opposite direction you are going to trade in order to trigger a signal. When the price crosses below the lower band, the signal dictates you buy in hopes that the price reverses upward.

This is the opposite of a momentum strategy. In the case of the Bollinger Band signal mentioned above, if the price continues its directional momentum at the time it generates the signal, the trade will lose money.

3.4 Volume-based Indicators

So far, we have only discussed indicators that depend on the history of past prices. For technical completeness, we will also discuss indicators that depend on other data, such as volume and candlestick data. Volume refers to the number of shares of an asset traded during a given time period. Candlestick data refers to the components the make up candlestick charts: the open, high, low, and closing prices for a period.

3.4.1 Chaikin Money Flow

The Chaikin Money Flow is an oscillator that depends on both volume and candlestick data. The formula is as follows, where y_t, h_t, l_t, and v_t represent the closing price, high price, low price, and volume, respectively. The variable q_t represents an intermediate calculation of the Chaikin Money Flow called the Money-Flow Volume.

$$q_t = \frac{(y_t - l_t) - (h_t - y_t)}{h_t - l_t} v_t = \frac{2y_t - h_t - l_t}{h_t - l_t} v_t$$

The Chaikin Money Flow (CMF), represented by z_t, for m periods, is then computed as follows.

$$z_t = \frac{\sum_{i=0}^{m-1} q_{t-i}}{\sum_{i=0}^{m-1} v_{t-i}}$$

To understand how the CMF works, we should study the properties of the term q_t. The fraction in q_t evaluates to 1 for $y_t = h_t$ and -1 for $y_t = l_t$. Further, the fraction in q_t evaluates to zero for $y_t = (h_t + l_t)/2$. So, z_t can be thought of as weighted average of volume, where the weights are determined by the positions of the closing prices relative the to the candlestick ranges. The resulting output z_t is bounded between -1 and 1.

The code is as follows.

```
def calculate_money_flow_volume_series(df: pd.DataFrame) -> pd.Series:
    """
    Calculates money flow series
    """
    mfv = df['volume'] * (2*df['close'] - df['high'] - df['low']) / \
                                    (df['high'] - df['low'])
    return mfv

def calculate_money_flow_volume(df: pd.DataFrame, n: int=20) -> pd.Series:
    """
    Calculates money flow volume, or q_t in our formula
    """
    return calculate_money_flow_volume_series(df).rolling(n).sum()

def calculate_chaikin_money_flow(df: pd.DataFrame, n: int=20) -> pd.Series:
    """
    Calculates the Chaikin money flow
    """
    return calculate_money_flow_volume(df, n) / df['volume'].rolling(n).sum()
```

Listing 3.6: Calculating Chaikin Money Flow

See Figure 3.6 for an example of the CMF on AWU.

The theory behind the CMF is that upside or downside buying pressure may reveal itself via volume activity before price moves occur. As such, the most compelling signal produced by the CMF is a divergence signal. Since the CMF indicator is volume-based, it attempts to identify instances where trading volume indicates a stock ought to go up or down in the future. For example, if an analyst sees the CMF going up while the stock price is going down, it could signal a reversal trade. Similarly, if an analyst sees a stock trading sideways while the CMF indicator is going up, it could signal a momentum or predictive trade.

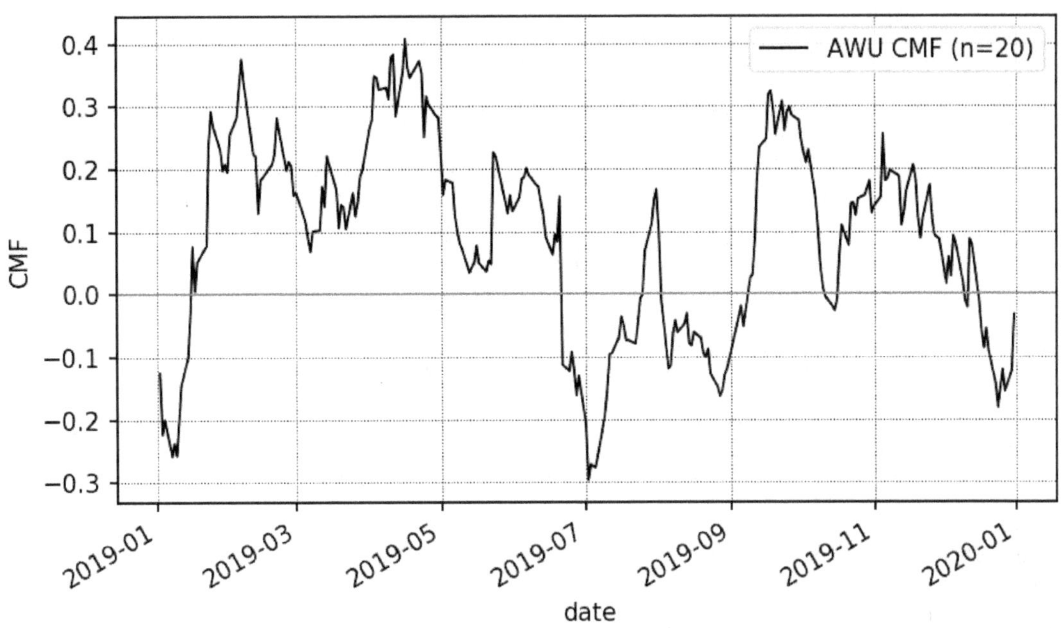

Figure 3.6: Chaikin Money Flow on AWU

3.5 Signals

We have provided a momentum investing signal example for the MACD and a reversal investing signal example for the Bollinger Bands. Many indicators can produce signals of both types, depending on how they are interpreted.

3.5.1 Data Structure of Signals

We have discussed how the data structure of indicators is typically parallel in size and structure to the underlying price history. The same is true for signals. If indicators are a date-indexed series of floating point values, signals can be thought of as a ternary series of $\{-1, 0, 1\}$, where -1 indicates selling, 0 indicates absence of a signal, and 1 indicates buying.

3.5.2 Generating Signals from Indicators

Turning technical indicators to signals is typically an exercise in boolean manipulation. The Listing 3.7 for example indicators creating the MACD and Bollinger Band indicators. The return value is a series consisting of values in $\{-1, 0, 1\}$ with the same date index as the input.

```
def create_macd_signal(series: pd.Series, n1: int=5, n2: int=34) -> pd.Series:
    """
    Create a momentum-based signal based on the MACD crossover principle.
    Generate a buy signal when the MACD cross above zero, and a sell signal when
    it crosses below zero.
    """
```

```
    # Calculate the macd and get the signs of the values.
    macd = calculate_macd_oscillator(series, n1, n2)
    macd_sign = np.sign(macd)

    # Create a copy shifted by some amount.
    macd_shifted_sign = macd_sign.shift(1, axis=0)

    # Multiply by the sign by the boolean. This will have the effect of casting
    # the boolean to an integer (either 0 or 1) and then multiply by the sign
    # (either -1, 0 or 1).
    return macd_sign * (macd_sign != macd_shifted_sign)


def create_bollinger_band_signal(series: pd.Series, n: int=20) -> pd.Series:
    """
    Create a reversal-based signal based on the upper and lower bands of the
    Bollinger bands. Generate a buy signal when the price is below the lower
    band, and a sell signal when the price is above the upper band.
    """
    bollinger_bands = calculate_bollinger_bands(series, n)
    sell = series > bollinger_bands['upper']
    buy = series < bollinger_bands['lower']
    return (1*buy - 1*sell)
```

Listing 3.7: Creating signals from indicators

As you can imagine, there are many possible signals that be generated from a single technical indicator.

3.5.3 The Perfect Indicator

A theoretically perfect indicator would produce signals that are always correct. If that is the case, why bother looking at common indicators like the MACD and Bollinger Bands? What would happen if we used both indicators at the same time? Further, if the MACD signal is momentum-based, and the Bollinger Bands signal is reversal-based, wouldn't they disagree with each other frequently?

The general answer to this question is that a momentum-based strategy will never work on a single asset all of the time, and neither will a reversal-based strategy. The task of generating the perfect series of signals can be generalized to not only developing a robust indicator, but also to determining when the underlying asset is in a momentum-based state or a reversal-based state. In other words, part of the task is determining whether the price of the underlying asset is trending upwards, downwards, or sideways. This will help determine whether or not a momentum-based or a reversal-based approach is appropriate. We will explore this idea further in the chapters on simulation and optimization.

3.5.4 Complex Indicators and Signals

To some extent, all quant shops, prop shops, and hedge funds are out to develop the so-called perfect signal. In doing so, they have pushed the limit in terms of the complexity and specificity of their indicators. If we think about a signal as simply a series of elements in the set $\{-1, 0, 1\}$, and we consider producing this signal to be the sole and primary job of quant traders, you can imagine how far a group of researchers might go to produce the best possible series.

It is possible to incorporate other data, even very messy and obscure data, into your signals. Major categories of data include fundamental data, analyst recommendations, order book data, and alternative data. Further, quant researchers can develop machine learning models to convert this data into signals. Later in this book, we will give a treatment of machine learning and alternative data, which can be extended to include virtually any source of data.

I am raising this point here in the book, because it is important to appreciate that a vast field of untapped opportunity lies within production of unique and complex signals. Complex signal generation is where the hard work and creativity of quant researchers can offer them a true market advantage.

3.6 Conclusion

In this chapter, we introduced readers to a few classes of indicators, discussed efficient time series functions, and gave examples of how to calculate some common indicators. We also started a discussion about complex signals and alternative data in practice. The next chapter will expand on these concepts by translating some of our indicators into a simulator that manages a portfolio of a selection of stocks across time.

Chapter 4

Simulation

This chapter will present a defensive and object-oriented approach to strategy simulation, otherwise referred to as backtesting. We will walk through the code for building a simulator for a multi-asset long-only strategy. We will pull in everything we have discussed thus far in the book.

Developing a good simulator is more of an issue of software development than quantitative finance. There are a lot of important software design decisions that have to be made if the simulator is to be functional, understandable, and fast.

4.1 Software Design Principles

This section will discuss the important software design principles that went into the design of the simulator.

4.1.1 Object-Oriented Programming (OOP)

A simulator is an excellent place to make use of object-oriented programming principles. We have broken up the simulator into three nesting parts.

The `Position` class holds information relevant to a single trade throughout its life. It can report on information relevant to single trades, and check that trading activity is not erroneously recorded.

The `PortfolioHistory` class holds a list of `Position` objects, records historical balances of cash, and reports on performance and behavior of the portfolio overall. It is also responsible for computing the equity curve, return series, and any performance metrics.

The `SimpleSimulator` class holds data about the prices, signals, and preferences of different stocks. It is primarily responsible for stepping through time, while managing `Position` objects and recording events in the `PortfolioHistory` object. This class will do the computational heavy lifting of looping through all of the data provided to it.

In order to write efficient and readable code, we will make liberal use of advanced Python programming features including decorators, static methods, properties, pseudo-private attributes, pass-by-reference, magic methods, and lambda functions. Readers will need a reasonable grasp on these concepts in order to understand the following code.

4.1.2 Defensive Programming

The `SimpleSimulator` class is responsible for managing multiple instances of the other two classes. As such, it is possible, and quite likely, that it will perform some undefined behavior at some point. Examples of undefined behavior could include the following.

- Opening and closing a position at the same instant.
- Recording the same position multiple times in the portfolio history.
- Recording an unclosed position.
- Recording cash and portfolio histories along different sets of dates.
- Having a negative cash balance.
- Having multiple positions open in the same asset at the same time.

Defensive programming is all about avoiding undefined behavior before it becomes a problem by guaranteeing that certain problematic events cannot occur without the program raising an exception.

In the spirit of defensive programming, readers will see numerous `assert` statements littered throughout the simulation code. These statements, if programmed carefully, are virtually free, and they allow us to proceed more confidently in writing code and analyzing simulation results.

In Python, `assert` statements raise an `AssertionError` exception when the expression following the `assert` keyword evaluates to `False`. Optionally, they can raise an error defined by a string when the assertion fails. If the assertion fails, you will see this error message in the console. See Listing 4.1 for an example.

```
assert 2 + 2 == 4, 'The laws of mathematics are crumbling.'
assert 2 + 2 == 5, 'You will see this message in an AssertionError.'
```

Listing 4.1: Assertions example

4.1.3 Classes as Interfaces

The `Position` and `PortfolioHistory` classes are designed as interfaces into underlying data structures that are managed and protected by efficient and defensive programming practices. In Python, it is a convention to treat class attributes and methods preceded by an underscore as *private* and to treat everything else as *public*.

In practice, this means that an attribute like `_logged_positions` should not be accessed directly by any code other than the class definition itself. The implication of the method being private is that any modification or use of the variable outside its own class methods are unsupported and may cause data integrity problems elsewhere in the object. If a user of the class would like to make sure a position appears in `_logged_positions`, he or she should call the `portfolio_simulator.add_to_history` method with the appropriate parameters, which also does a handful of other things with different variables. Making sure we only access public methods and attributes while programming and modifying the simulator ensures that we do not encounter any undefined behavior.

Note that Python itself does not acknowledge any difference between public and private variables for sake of assignment and access. It would be perfectly valid Python to write `portfolio_simulator._logged_positions = 'total_nonsense'`, but it would not be good practice for a number of reasons. It would also certainly cause errors because `_logged_positions` is assumed to be of type `Set[Position]` throughout.

4.1.4 Compute-time Optimization

We use some fancy `pandas` tricks in the simulator code in order to minimize runtime. The most significant trick we use involves hierarchical data frames and `pd.DataFrame.itertuples()`.

There are a few options for looping through data frames in `pandas`, including `df.iterrows()`, `df.itertuples()`, and something involving `for i in df.index`. While all of the aforementioned methods have the same time complexity ($O(nm)$ for n rows and m columns), the `df.itertuples()` method is the fastest by a factor of about 10, especially on large data frames. It has similar runtime characteristics to looping through a raw numerical matrix, while still maintaining some semblance of column names known by the data frame.

Additionally, while `pandas` indexes have $O(1)$ lookup time and are set-like, lookups are slow in practice. Thus, it is very important that the data frame you are looping through contains all of the data-frame-like data you wish to work with inside the loop. This is why we chose to wrangle with hierarchical data frames. If this topic interests you, please see `pypm.data_io.concatenate_metrics` for our approach to dynamically constructing hierarchical data frames. For now, readers are encouraged to focus on understanding the simulation logic rather than the implementation details.

4.2 Building a Simulator

This section will walk readers through development of a trading strategy simulator in Python.

4.2.1 Defining Supported Behavior and Constraints

As we will discuss later in this chapter, simulators are not well-suited for generalization. It is typically best to define a set of supported behaviors and constraints upon which to design your simulator. We have mentioned previously that we intend to build a multi-asset long-only trading strategy. It will support the following.

- The strategy will open and close long positions on a fixed maximum number of distinct assets simultaneously.
  - Entry and exit dates can be asynchronous.
  - The number of shares held of each asset will be fixed over the length of the trade.
  - Cash will be divided equally among available opportunities at time of purchase.
  - Purchase of fractional shares is allowed for mathematical simplicity.
- The simulator will support fees and slippage.
  - A fixed trade fee is supported. It will be charged once to the cash balance upon purchase, but not sale, of an asset.
  - A percentage slippage amount is supported. The percentage slippage will be applied adversely to the portfolio on both purchase and sale of an asset.
- The input data will consist of three date-indexed data frames with column names representing the assets under consideration.
  - `price` will be a data frame of closing prices.
  - `signal` will be a data frame with integers in the set $\{-1, 0, 1\}$, where -1 represents a sell signal, 0 represents no signal, and 1 represents a buy signal.
  - `preference` will be a data frame of floats representing relative preference for each symbol at any point in time, which may be entirely independent from the signal. The preferences will be used to determine which assets are bought or swapped out in the case of many concurrent buy signals.
  - The input data is assumed to have null values at the beginning of a series, but a non-null series cannot become null once it is in play, as the simulator moves forward in time. In other words, stocks can be listed, but not delisted, during the simulation time frame.

4.2.2 Defining a Position Object

The `Position` class and a `position` object are defined as follows.

```
import pandas as pd
import matplotlib.pyplot as plt
```

```
from typing import Tuple, List, Dict, Callable, NewType, Any
from collections import OrderedDict, defaultdict

from pypm import metrics, signals, data_io

Symbol = NewType('Symbol', str)
Dollars = NewType('Dollars', float)

DATE_FORMAT_STR = '%a %b %d, %Y'
def _pdate(date: pd.Timestamp):
    """Pretty-print a datetime with just the date"""
    return date.strftime(DATE_FORMAT_STR)

class Position(object):
    """
    A simple object to hold and manipulate data related to long stock trades.

    Allows a single buy and sell operation on an asset for a constant number of
    shares.

    The __init__ method is equivelant to a buy operation. The exit
    method is a sell operation.
    """

    def __init__(self, symbol: Symbol, entry_date: pd.Timestamp,
        entry_price: Dollars, shares: int):
        """
        Equivelent to buying a certain number of shares of the asset
        """

        # Recorded on initialization
        self.entry_date = entry_date
        self.entry_price = entry_price
        self.shares = shares
        self.symbol = symbol

        # Recorded on position exit
        self.exit_date: pd.Timestamp = None
        self.exit_price: Dollars = None

        # For easily getting current portolio value
        self.last_date: pd.Timestamp = None
        self.last_price: Dollars = None

        # Updated intermediately
        self._dict_series: Dict[pd.Timestamp, Dollars] = OrderedDict()
        self.record_price_update(entry_date, entry_price)

        # Cache control for pd.Series representation
        self._price_series: pd.Series = None
        self._needs_update_pd_series: bool = True

    def exit(self, exit_date, exit_price):
```

```
        """
        Equivelent to selling a stock holding
        """
        assert self.entry_date != exit_date, 'Churned a position same-day.'
        assert not self.exit_date, 'Position already closed.'
        self.record_price_update(exit_date, exit_price)
        self.exit_date = exit_date
        self.exit_price = exit_price

    def record_price_update(self, date, price):
        """
        Stateless function to record intermediate prices of existing positions
        """
        self.last_date = date
        self.last_price = price
        self._dict_series[date] = price

        # Invalidate cache on self.price_series
        self._needs_update_pd_series = True

    @property
    def price_series(self) -> pd.Series:
        """
        Returns cached readonly pd.Series
        """
        if self._needs_update_pd_series or self._price_series is None:
            self._price_series = pd.Series(self._dict_series)
            self._needs_update_pd_series = False
        return self._price_series

    @property
    def last_value(self) -> Dollars:
        return self.last_price * self.shares

    @property
    def is_active(self) -> bool:
        return self.exit_date is None

    @property
    def is_closed(self) -> bool:
        return not self.is_active

    @property
    def value_series(self) -> pd.Series:
        """
        Returns the value of the position over time. Ignores self.exit_date.
        Used in calculating the equity curve.
        """
        assert self.is_closed, 'Position must be closed to access this property'
        return self.shares * self.price_series[:-1]

    @property
    def percent_return(self) -> float:
        return (self.exit_price / self.entry_price) - 1
```

```
    @property
    def entry_value(self) -> Dollars:
        return self.shares * self.entry_price

    @property
    def exit_value(self) -> Dollars:
        return self.shares * self.exit_price

    @property
    def change_in_value(self) -> Dollars:
        return self.exit_value - self.entry_value

    @property
    def trade_length(self):
        return len(self._dict_series) - 1

    def print_position_summary(self):
        _entry_date = _pdate(self.entry_date)
        _exit_date = _pdate(self.exit_date)
        _days = self.trade_length

        _entry_price = round(self.entry_price, 2)
        _exit_price = round(self.exit_price, 2)

        _entry_value = round(self.entry_value, 2)
        _exit_value = round(self.exit_value, 2)

        _return = round(100 * self.percent_return, 1)
        _diff = round(self.change_in_value, 2)

        print(f'{self.symbol:<5}     Trade summary')
        print(f'Date:     {_entry_date} -> {_exit_date} [{_days} days]')
        print(f'Price:    ${_entry_price} -> ${_exit_price} [{_return}%]')
        print(f'Value:    ${_entry_value} -> ${_exit_value} [${_diff}]')
        print()

    def __hash__(self):
        """
        A unique position will be defined by a unique combination of an
        entry_date and symbol, in accordance with our constraints regarding
        duplicate, variable, and compound positions
        """
        return hash((self.entry_date, self.symbol))
```

Listing 4.2: Position class definition

Listing 4.2 is about 150 lines of code, and represents about 25% of all of the financial logic built into our simulator. It is worth spending some time studying this class definition, because the `Position` class represents all of the useful financial computations that be performed given only the knowledge of a stock symbol, start date, end date, and all of the closing prices in between those dates. As such, we can do some interesting experiments and test calculations using only this class. See Listing 4.3 for an example of using the `Position` class. Figure 4.1 shows `position.price_series` plotted over AWU closing prices.

```
import pandas as pd
```

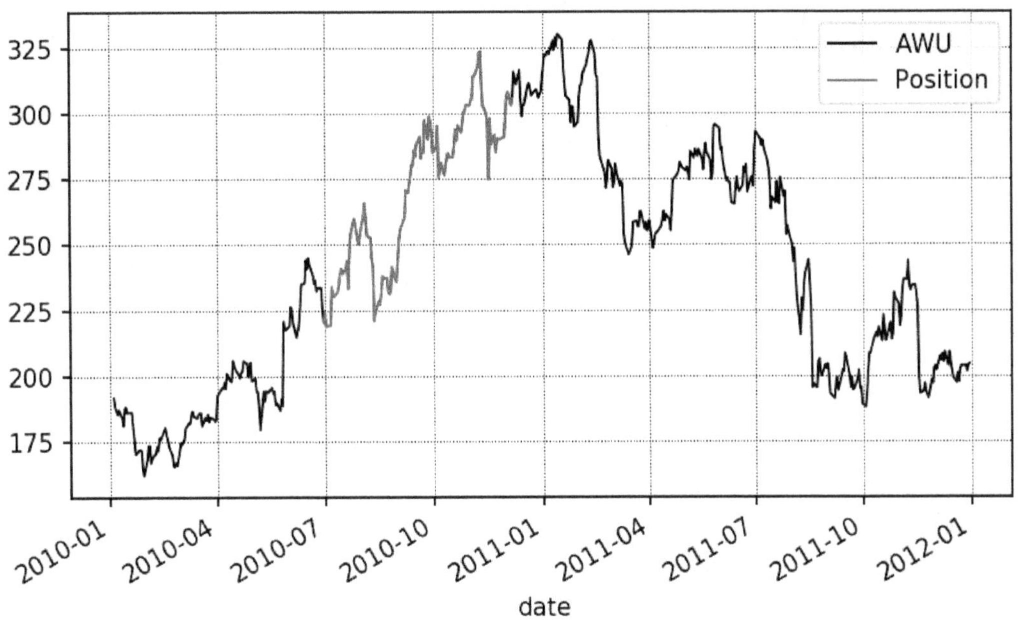

Figure 4.1: Position data on AWU

```
from pypm import data_io, portfolio

symbol = 'AWU'
df = data_io.load_eod_data(symbol)
shares_to_buy = 50

for i, row in enumerate(df.itertuples()):
    date = row.Index
    price = row.close

    if i == 123:
        position = portfolio.Position(symbol, date, price, shares_to_buy)
    elif 123 < i < 234:
        position.record_price_update(date, price)
    elif i == 234:
        position.exit(date, price)

position.print_position_summary()

# Returns ...
# AWU         Trade summary
# Date:       Wed Jun 30, 2010 -> Tue Dec 07, 2010 [111 days]
# Price:      $220.34 -> $305.98 [38.9%]
# Value:      $11017.0 -> $15299.0 [$4282.0]
```

Listing 4.3: Position object usage

Note all the features the `Position` class has currently. We have already arrived at a reasonably clean interface for recording information about stock holdings over time, and we haven't even introduced the concept of a portfolio or a simulation to our code.

4.2.3 Defining a Portfolio History Object

The next class we will define is called the `PortfolioHistory`. This class will primarily be an organized container for position objects. With those position objects, it will be able to derive the equity curve and numerous performance metrics.

```
class PortfolioHistory(object):
    """
    Holds Position objects and keeps track of portfolio variables.
    Produces summary statistics.
    """

    def __init__(self):
        # Keep track of positions, recorded in this list after close
        self.position_history: List[Position] = []
        self._logged_positions: Set[Position] = set()

        # Keep track of the last seen date
        self.last_date: pd.Timestamp = pd.Timestamp.min

        # Readonly fields
        self._cash_history: Dict[pd.Timestamp, Dollars] = dict()
        self._simulation_finished = False
        self._spy: pd.DataFrame = pd.DataFrame()
        self._spy_log_returns: pd.Series = pd.Series()

    def add_to_history(self, position: Position):
        _log = self._logged_positions
        assert not position in _log, 'Recorded the same position twice.'
        assert position.is_closed, 'Position is not closed.'
        self._logged_positions.add(position)
        self.position_history.append(position)
        self.last_date = max(self.last_date, position.last_date)

    def record_cash(self, date, cash):
        self._cash_history[date] = cash
        self.last_date = max(self.last_date, date)

    @staticmethod
    def _as_oseries(d: Dict[pd.Timestamp, Any]) -> pd.Series:
        return pd.Series(d).sort_index()

    def _compute_cash_series(self):
        self._cash_series = self._as_oseries(self._cash_history)

    @property
    def cash_series(self) -> pd.Series:
        return self._cash_series

    def _compute_portfolio_value_series(self):
        value_by_date = defaultdict(float)
        last_date = self.last_date
```

```
        # Add up value of assets
        for position in self.position_history:
            for date, value in position.value_series.items():
                value_by_date[date] += value

        # Make sure all dates in cash_series are present
        for date in self.cash_series.index:
            value_by_date[date] += 0

        self._portfolio_value_series = self._as_oseries(value_by_date)

    @property
    def portfolio_value_series(self):
        return self._portfolio_value_series

    def _compute_equity_series(self):
        c_series = self.cash_series
        p_series = self.portfolio_value_series
        assert all(c_series.index == p_series.index), \
            'portfolio_series has dates not in cash_series'
        self._equity_series = c_series + p_series

    @property
    def equity_series(self):
        return self._equity_series

    def _compute_log_return_series(self):
        self._log_return_series = \
            metrics.calculate_log_return_series(self.equity_series)

    @property
    def log_return_series(self):
        return self._log_return_series

    def _assert_finished(self):
        assert self._simulation_finished, \
            'Simuation must be finished by running self.finish() in order ' + \
            'to access this method or property.'

    def finish(self):
        """
        Notate that the simulation is finished and compute readonly values
        """
        self._simulation_finished = True
        self._compute_cash_series()
        self._compute_portfolio_value_series()
        self._compute_equity_series()
        self._compute_log_return_series()
        self._assert_finished()

    def compute_portfolio_size_series(self) -> pd.Series:
        size_by_date = defaultdict(int)
        for position in self.position_history:
```

```
            for date in position.value_series.index:
                size_by_date[date] += 1
        return self._as_oseries(size_by_date)

    @property
    def spy(self):
        if self._spy.empty:
            self._spy = data_io.load_spy_data()
        return self._spy

    @property
    def spy_log_returns(self):
        if self._spy_log_returns.empty:
            close = self.spy['close']
            self._spy_log_returns =  metrics.calculate_log_return_series(close)
        return self._spy_log_returns

    @property
    def percent_return(self):
        return metrics.calculate_percent_return(self.equity_series)

    @property
    def spy_percent_return(self):
        return metrics.calculate_percent_return(self.spy['close'])

    @property
    def cagr(self):
        return metrics.calculate_cagr(self.equity_series)

    @property
    def volatility(self):
        return metrics.calculate_annualized_volatility(self.log_return_series)

    @property
    def sharpe_ratio(self):
        return metrics.calculate_sharpe_ratio(self.equity_series)

    @property
    def spy_cagr(self):
        return metrics.calculate_cagr(self.spy['close'])

    @property
    def excess_cagr(self):
        return self.cagr - self.spy_cagr

    @property
    def jensens_alpha(self):
        return metrics.calculate_jensens_alpha(
            self.log_return_series,
            self.spy_log_returns,
        )

    @property
    def dollar_max_drawdown(self):
```

```
        return metrics.calculate_max_drawdown(self.equity_series, 'dollar')

    @property
    def percent_max_drawdown(self):
        return metrics.calculate_max_drawdown(self.equity_series, 'percent')

    @property
    def log_max_drawdown_ratio(self):
        return metrics.calculate_log_max_drawdown_ratio(self.equity_series)

    @property
    def number_of_trades(self):
        return len(self.position_history)

    @property
    def average_active_trades(self):
        return self.compute_portfolio_size_series().mean()

    @property
    def final_cash(self):
        self._assert_finished()
        return self.cash_series[-1]

    @property
    def final_equity(self):
        self._assert_finished()
        return self.equity_series[-1]

    def print_position_summaries(self):
        for position in self.position_history:
            position.print_position_summary()

    def print_summary(self):
        self._assert_finished()
        s = f'Equity: ${self.final_equity:.2f}\n' \
            f'Percent Return: {100*self.percent_return:.2f}%\n' \
            f'S&P 500 Return: {100*self.spy_percent_return:.2f}%\n\n' \
            f'Number of trades: {self.number_of_trades}\n' \
            f'Average active trades: {self.average_active_trades:.2f}\n\n' \
            f'CAGR: {100*self.cagr:.2f}%\n' \
            f'S&P 500 CAGR: {100*self.spy_cagr:.2f}%\n' \
            f'Excess CAGR: {100*self.excess_cagr:.2f}%\n\n' \
            f'Annualized Volatility: {100*self.volatility:.2f}%\n' \
            f'Sharpe Ratio: {self.sharpe_ratio:.2f}\n' \
            f'Jensen\'s Alpha: {self.jensens_alpha:.6f}\n\n' \
            f'Dollar Max Drawdown: ${self.dollar_max_drawdown:.2f}\n' \
            f'Percent Max Drawdown: {100*self.percent_max_drawdown:.2f}%\n' \
            f'Log Max Drawdown Ratio: {self.log_max_drawdown_ratio:.2f}\n'

        print(s)

    def plot(self, show=True) -> plt.Figure:
        """
        Plots equity, cash and portfolio value curves.
```

```
        """
        self._assert_finished()

        figure, axes = plt.subplots(nrows=3, ncols=1)
        figure.tight_layout(pad=3.0)
        axes[0].plot(self.equity_series)
        axes[0].set_title('Equity')
        axes[0].grid()

        axes[1].plot(self.cash_series)
        axes[1].set_title('Cash')
        axes[1].grid()

        axes[2].plot(self.portfolio_value_series)
        axes[2].set_title('Portfolio Value')
        axes[2].grid()

        if show:
            plt.show()

        return figure
```

Listing 4.4: Portfolio history class definition

There is a lot going on here, and it is not essential that readers understand every bit of it in order to draw value from this book. We will go through some important features of the `PortfolioHistory` class below.

Note how few public methods are available in the class definition. The public methods include `add_to_history`, `record_cash`, `finish`, `print_position_summaries`, `print_summary`, and `plot`. In other words, the three main things you will do with this class are initializing it, recording cash balances, and recording closed positions. The rest of the things you will do with this class involve summary, investigation, and reporting.

Readers will notice there are many public properties in this class, consisting mainly of readonly data and performance metrics. It will be important in the next chapter on optimization that these performance metrics are easily accessible.

See Listing 4.5 for an example using the `PortfolioHistory` class. It is very similar to the prior listing using the `Position` object, except that it does some additional housekeeping to record the history of cash holdings and closed positions. The result is a significant expansion of reporting and plotting features from what the `Position` object provided. The Figure 4.2 for the output of the plot.

```
import pandas as pd
from pypm import data_io
from pypm.portfolio import Position, PortfolioHistory

symbol = 'AWU'
df = data_io.load_eod_data(symbol)

portfolio_history = PortfolioHistory()
initial_cash = cash = 10000

for i, row in enumerate(df.itertuples()):
    date = row.Index
    price = row.close

    if i == 123:
```

```
        # Figure out how many shares to buy
        shares_to_buy = initial_cash / price

        # Record the position
        position = Position(symbol, date, price, shares_to_buy)

        # Spend all of your cash
        cash -= initial_cash

    elif 123 < i < 2345:
        position.record_price_update(date, price)

    elif i == 2345:
        # Sell the asset
        position.exit(date, price)

        # Get your cash back
        cash += price * shares_to_buy

        # Record the position
        portfolio_history.add_to_history(position)

    # Record cash at every step
    portfolio_history.record_cash(date, cash)

portfolio_history.finish()

portfolio_history.print_position_summaries()
# Returns ...
# AWU       Trade summary
# Date:     Wed Jun 30, 2010 -> Tue Apr 30, 2019 [2222 days]
# Price:    $220.34 -> $386.26 [75.3%]
# Value:    $10000.0 -> $17530.18 [$7530.18]

portfolio_history.print_summary()
# Returns ...
# Equity: $17530.18
# Percent Return: 75.30%
# S&P 500 Return: 184.00%
#
# Number of trades: 1
# Average active trades: 1.00
#
# CAGR: 5.78%
# S&P 500 CAGR: 11.02%
# Excess CAGR: -5.24%
#
# Annualized Volatility: 29.97%
# Sharpe Ratio: 0.19
# Jensen's Alpha: -0.000198
#
# Dollar Max Drawdown: $9006.08
# Percent Max Drawdown: 60.08%
# Log Max Drawdown Ratio: -0.36
```

```
portfolio_history.plot()
```

Listing 4.5: Portfolio history object usage

4.2.4 Defining a Simulator

In Listings 4.3 and 4.5, we showed simple examples using the `Position` and `PortfolioHistory` classes. Those listings were essentially a trivial simulator. The `SimpleSimulator` class will look very similar to those listings, the main difference being that it handles portfolios with multiple assets. See Listing 4.6 for our implementation of the `SimpleSimulator`.

```
from typing import Tuple, List, Dict, Callable, NewType, Any, Iterable

import pandas as pd
import matplotlib.pyplot as plt

from pypm import metrics, signals, data_io
from pypm.portfolio import PortfolioHistory, Position, Symbol, Dollars

from collections import OrderedDict, defaultdict

class SimpleSimulator(object):
    """
    A simple trading simulator to work with the PortfolioHistory class
    """

    def __init__(self, initial_cash: float=10000, max_active_positions: int=5,
        percent_slippage: float=0.0005, trade_fee: float=1):

        ### Set simulation parameters

        # Initial cash in porfolio
        # self.cash will fluctuate
        self.initial_cash = self.cash = initial_cash

        # Maximum number of different assets that can be help simultaneously
        self.max_active_positions: int = max_active_positions

        # The percentage difference between closing price and fill price for the
        # position, to simulate adverse effects of market orders
        self.percent_slippage = percent_slippage

        # The fixed fee in order to open a position in dollar terms
        self.trade_fee = trade_fee

        # Keep track of live trades
        self.active_positions_by_symbol: Dict[Symbol, Position] = OrderedDict()

        # Keep track of portfolio history like cash, equity, and positions
        self.portfolio_history = PortfolioHistory()

    @property
    def active_positions_count(self):
```

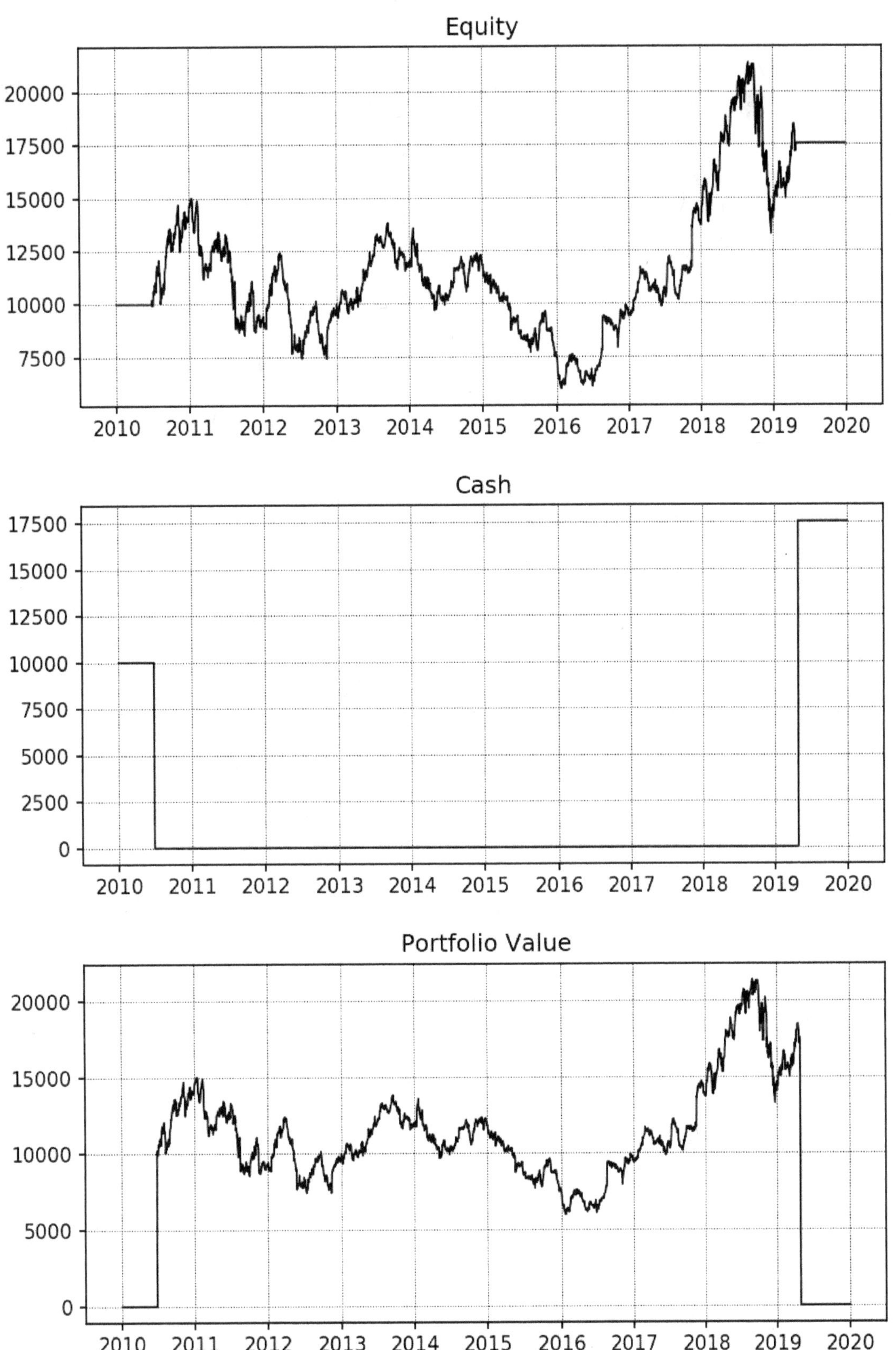

Figure 4.2: Portfolio History for AWU Example

```
        return len(self.active_positions_by_symbol)

    @property
    def free_position_slots(self):
        return self.max_active_positions - self.active_positions_count

    @property
    def active_symbols(self) -> List[Symbol]:
        return list(self.active_positions_by_symbol.keys())

    def print_initial_parameters(self):
        s = f'Initial Cash: ${self.initial_cash} \n' \
            f'Maximum Number of Assets: {self.max_active_positions}\n'
        print(s)
        return s

    @staticmethod
    def make_tuple_lookup(columns) -> Callable[[str, str], int]:
        """
        Map a multi-index dataframe to an itertuples-like object.

        The index of the dateframe is always the zero-th element.
        """

        # col is a hierarchical column index represented by a tuple of strings
        tuple_lookup: Dict[Tuple[str, str], int] = {
            col: i + 1 for i, col in enumerate(columns)
        }

        return lambda symbol, metric: tuple_lookup[(symbol, metric)]

    @staticmethod
    def make_all_valid_lookup(_idx: Callable):
        """
        Return a function that checks for valid data, given a lookup function
        """
        return lambda row, symbol: (
            not pd.isna(row[_idx(symbol, 'pref')]) and \
            not pd.isna(row[_idx(symbol, 'signal')]) and \
            not pd.isna(row[_idx(symbol, 'price')])
        )

    def buy_to_open(self, symbol, date, price):
        """
        Keep track of new position, make sure it isn't an existing position.
        Verify you have cash.
        """

        # Figure out how much we are willing to spend
        cash_to_spend = self.cash / self.free_position_slots
        cash_to_spend -= self.trade_fee

        # Calculate buy_price and number of shares. Fractional shares allowed.
        purchase_price = (1 + self.percent_slippage) * price
```

```
        shares = cash_to_spend / purchase_price

        # Spend the cash
        self.cash -= cash_to_spend + self.trade_fee
        assert self.cash >= 0, 'Spent cash you do not have.'
        self.portfolio_history.record_cash(date, self.cash)

        # Record the position
        positions_by_symbol = self.active_positions_by_symbol
        assert not symbol in positions_by_symbol, 'Symbol already in portfolio.'
        position = Position(symbol, date, purchase_price, shares)
        positions_by_symbol[symbol] = position

    def sell_to_close(self, symbol, date, price):
        """
        Keep track of exit price, recover cash, close position, and record it in
        portfolio history.

        Will raise a KeyError if symbol isn't an active position
        """

        # Exit the position
        positions_by_symbol = self.active_positions_by_symbol
        position = positions_by_symbol[symbol]
        position.exit(date, price)

        # Receive the cash
        sale_value = position.last_value * (1 - self.percent_slippage)
        self.cash += sale_value
        self.portfolio_history.record_cash(date, self.cash)

        # Record in portfolio history
        self.portfolio_history.add_to_history(position)
        del positions_by_symbol[symbol]

    @staticmethod
    def _assert_equal_columns(*args: Iterable[pd.DataFrame]):
        column_names = set(args[0].columns.values)
        for arg in args[1:]:
            assert set(arg.columns.values) == column_names, \
                'Found unequal column names in input data frames.'

    def simulate(self, price: pd.DataFrame, signal: pd.DataFrame,
        preference: pd.DataFrame):
        """
        Runs the simulation.

        price, signal, and preference are data frames with the column names
        represented by the same set of stock symbols.
        """

        # Create a hierarchical data frame to loop through
        self._assert_equal_columns(price, signal, preference)
        df = data_io.concatenate_metrics({
```

```
        'price': price,
        'signal': signal,
        'pref': preference,
    })

    # Get list of symbols
    all_symbols = list(set(price.columns.values))

    # Get lookup functions
    _idx = self.make_tuple_lookup(df.columns)
    _all_valid = self.make_all_valid_lookup(_idx)

    # Store some variables
    active_positions_by_symbol = self.active_positions_by_symbol
    max_active_positions = self.max_active_positions

    # Iterating over all dates.
    # itertuples() is significantly faster than iterrows(), it however comes
    # at the cost of being able index easily. In order to get around this
    # we use an tuple lookup function: "_idx"
    for row in df.itertuples():

        # date index is always first element of tuple row
        date = row[0]

        # Get symbols with valid and tradable data
        symbols: List[str] = [s for s in all_symbols if _all_valid(row, s)]

        # Iterate over active positions and sell stocks with a sell signal.
        _active = self.active_symbols
        to_exit = [s for s in _active if row[_idx(s, 'signal')] == -1]
        for s in to_exit:
            sell_price = row[_idx(s, 'price')]
            self.sell_to_close(s, date, sell_price)

        # Get up to max_active_positions symbols with a buy signal in
        # decreasing order of preference
        to_buy = [
            s for s in symbols if \
                row[_idx(s, 'signal')] == 1 and \
                not s in active_positions_by_symbol
        ]
        to_buy.sort(key=lambda s: row[_idx(s, 'pref')], reverse=True)
        to_buy = to_buy[:max_active_positions]

        for s in to_buy:
            buy_price = row[_idx(s, 'price')]
            buy_preference = row[_idx(s, 'pref')]

            # If we have some empty slots, just buy the asset outright
            if self.active_positions_count < max_active_positions:
                self.buy_to_open(s, date, buy_price)
                continue
```

```
                # If are holding max_active_positions, evaluate a swap based on
                # preference
                _active = self.active_symbols
                active_prefs = [(s, row[_idx(s, 'pref')]) for s in _active]

                _min = min(active_prefs, key=lambda k: k[1])
                min_active_symbol, min_active_preference = _min

                # If a more preferable symbol exists, then sell an old one
                if min_active_preference < buy_preference:
                    sell_price = row[_idx(min_active_symbol, 'price')]
                    self.sell_to_close(min_active_symbol, date, sell_price)
                    self.buy_to_open(s, date, buy_price)

            # Update price data everywhere
            for s in self.active_symbols:
                price = row[_idx(s, 'price')]
                position = active_positions_by_symbol[s]
                position.record_price_update(date, price)

        # Sell all positions and mark simulation as complete
        for s in self.active_symbols:
            self.sell_to_close(s, date, row[_idx(s, 'price')])
        self.portfolio_history.finish()
```

Listing 4.6: Simple simulator class definition

See Listing 4.7 for example usage of SimpleSimulator. See Figure 4.3 for the output.

```
### pypm/simulate_portfolio.py
from pypm import metrics, signals, data_io, simulation
import pandas as pd

def simulate_portfolio():

    bollinger_n = 20
    sharpe_n = 20

    # Load in data
    symbols: List[str] = data_io.get_all_symbols()
    prices: pd.DataFrame = data_io.load_eod_matrix(symbols)

    # Use the bollinger band outer band crossorver as a signal
    _bollinger = signals.create_bollinger_band_signal
    signal = prices.apply(_bollinger, args=(bollinger_n,), axis=0)

    # Use a rolling sharpe ratio approximation as a preference matrix
    _sharpe = metrics.calculate_rolling_sharpe_ratio
    preference = prices.apply(_sharpe, args=(sharpe_n, ), axis=0)

    # Run the simulator
    simulator = simulation.SimpleSimulator(
        initial_cash=10000,
        max_active_positions=5,
        percent_slippage=0.0005,
```

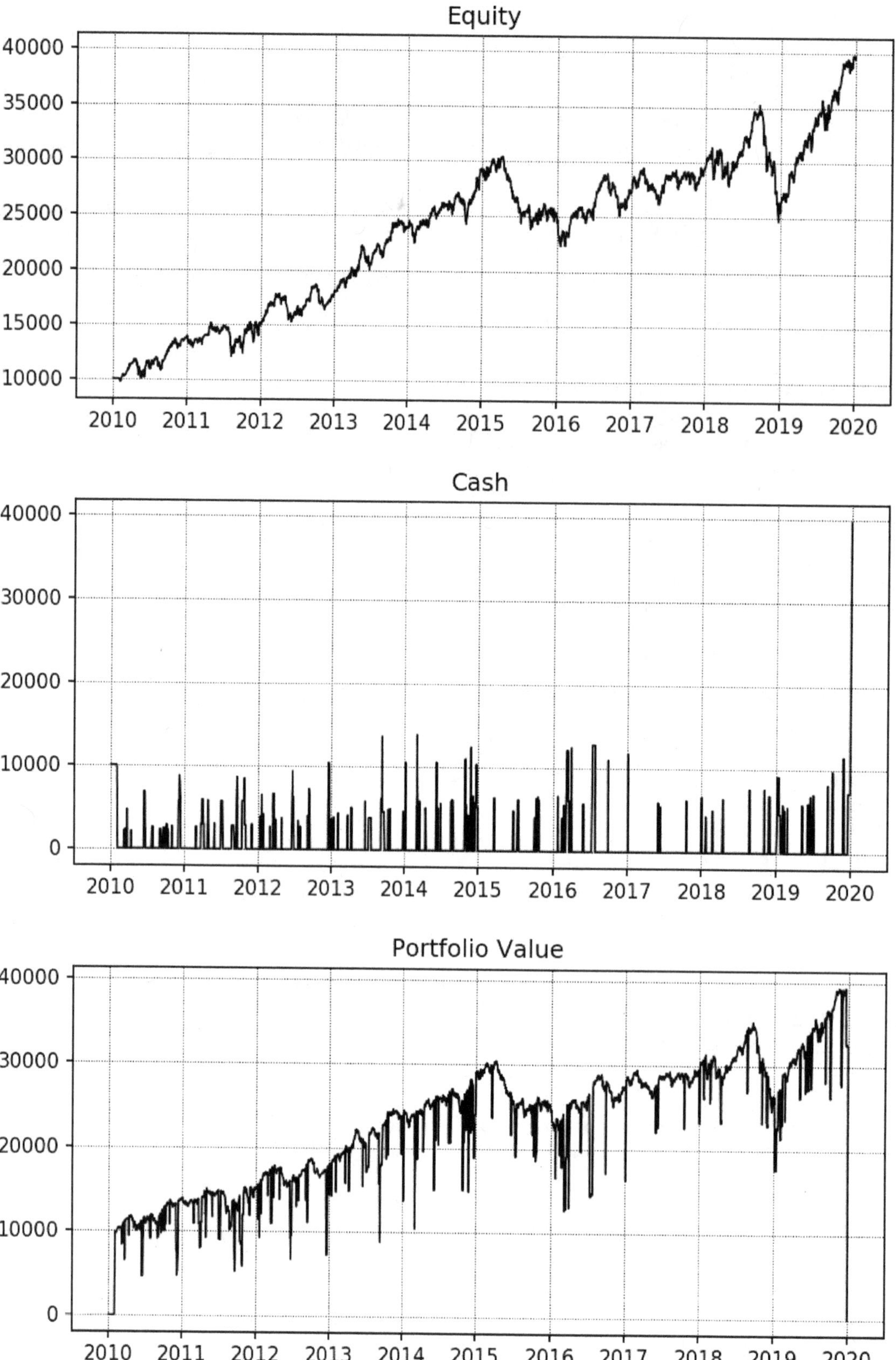

Figure 4.3: Multi-asset Portfolio Simulation Example

```
        trade_fee=1,
    )
    simulator.simulate(prices, signal, preference)

    # Print results
    simulator.portfolio_history.print_position_summaries()
    simulator.print_initial_parameters()
    simulator.portfolio_history.print_summary()
    simulator.portfolio_history.plot()

if __name__ == '__main__':
    simulate_portfolio()

# Returns ...
# Initial Cash: $10000
# Maximum Number of Assets: 5
#
# Equity: $39758.61
# Percent Return: 297.59%
# S&P 500 Return: 184.00%
#
# Number of trades: 1835
# Average active trades: 4.83
#
# CAGR: 14.82%
# S&P 500 CAGR: 11.02%
# Excess CAGR: 3.80%
#
# Annualized Volatility: 17.93%
# Sharpe Ratio: 0.83
# Jensen's Alpha: 0.000147
#
# Dollar Max Drawdown: $10594.83
# Percent Max Drawdown: 30.03%
# Log Max Drawdown Ratio: 1.02
```

Listing 4.7: Simple simulator example usage

Note from the terminal output in Listing 4.7 how our Bollinger Bands and Rolling Sharpe Ratio strategy performed. It outperforms the S&P 500 on a CAGR basis, but it did not achieve a high Jensen's Alpha. The low Jensen's Alpha here is evidence that the performance achieved by this strategy was similar to that of a leveraged long position on the S&P 500. See Figure 4.4 for visual support of this.

4.3 Simulator Experiments

Now that we have defined a simulator, we can start experimenting with it to learn how different variables affect the performance of the simulated portfolio. For example, readers might be immediately curious how different fee structures and indicator parameters affect the overall performance. We can now answer questions such as the following. "Which value of `max_active_positions` maximizes the simulated performance for a given strategy?"

Note that the results of these simulations are in no way trading recommendations or definitive statements about how these strategies will perform in the future. The reason we will experiment with and tweak

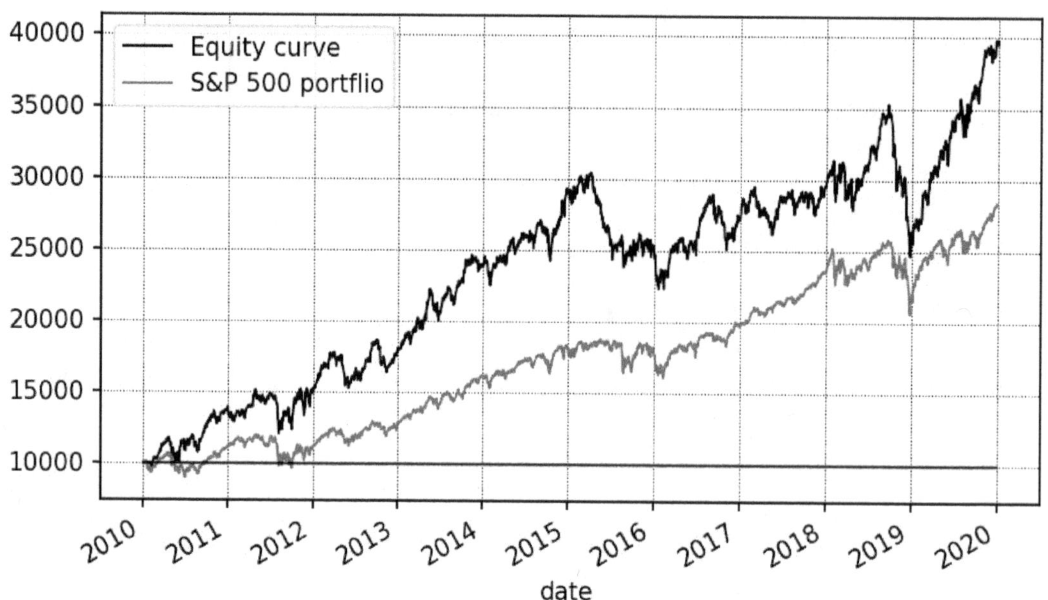

Figure 4.4: Multi-asset portfolio vs. Benchmark

simulation parameters is to learn. The knowledge we gain from tweaking the parameters helps us develop an intuitive understanding of the dynamics of financial trading, both in algorithmic and discretionary contexts.

In this section, we will tweak the simulator parameters along a single axis while keeping the other values constant at their defaults.

4.3.1 Tweaking Indicator Parameters

There are two important indicators we use in this strategy: the Bollinger Bands and the Rolling Sharpe Ratio. Both of these have default values of 20 for their window length parameter.

See Figures 4.5 and 4.6 for the excess CAGR and Jensen's Alpha against the Bollinger Band length. We see that the portfolio underperforms the market for a vast majority of alternative Bollinger Band values above 30, though is an interesting trough near 350.

As we mentioned earlier, the success of this strategy seems to simulate a higher leverage investment in the S&P 500. The Jensen's Alpha plot in Figure 4.6 confirms this, as there is no value of Jensen's Alpha that is significantly above zero.

See Figure 4.7 for the excess CAGR against the Rolling Sharp Ratio length. Keep in mind that the Rolling Sharpe Ratio in this strategy is used to determine which assets we would prefer to buy when there is an overabundance of buy signals. We see there is a significant peak around 80 in the plot, suggesting that assets with a medium-term high Sharpe ratio should be the most preferred investments in this strategy.

4.3.2 Tweaking Simulation Parameters

In our `SimpleSimulator` class, we support some basic simulation parameters regarding trading fees and number of positions that can be held at one time. We will tweak those parameters to study their impact on

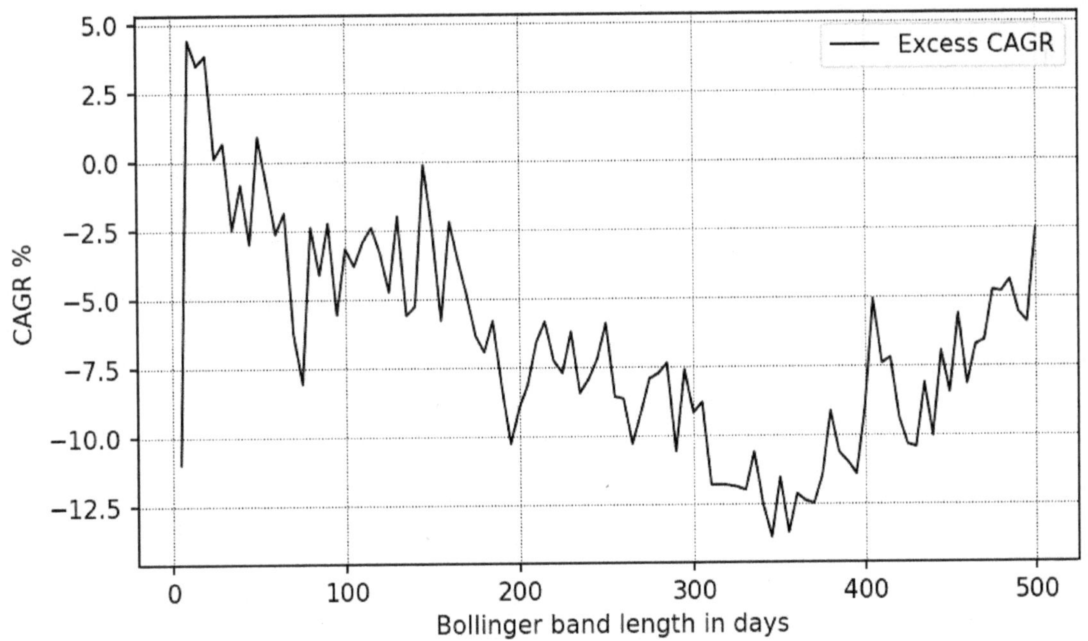

Figure 4.5: Excess CAGR by Bollinger Band Length

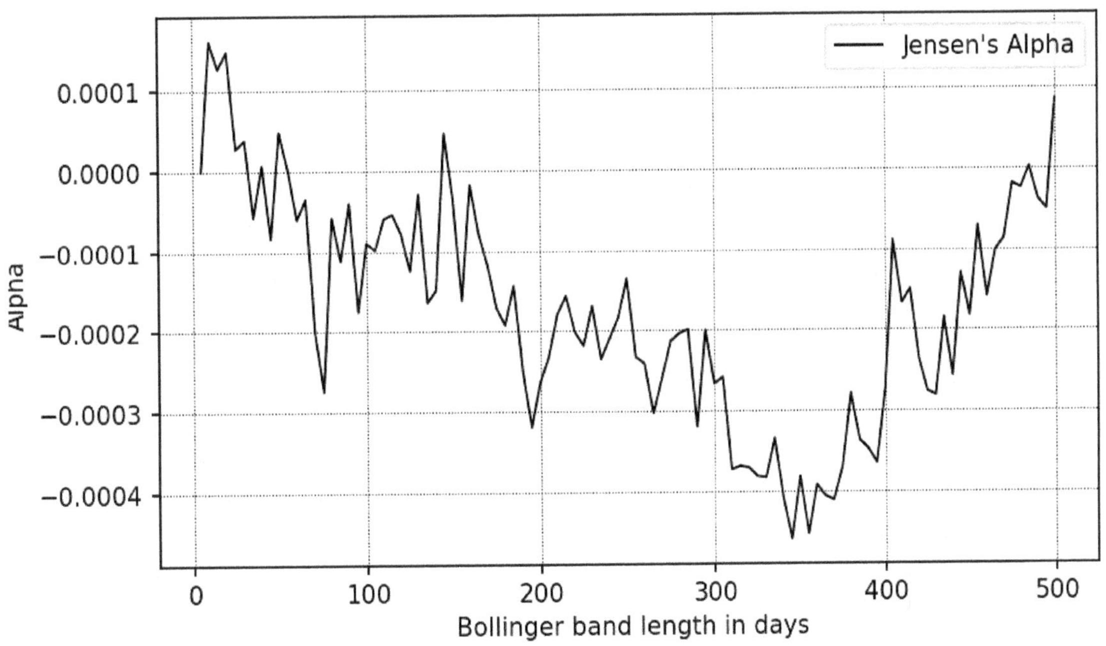

Figure 4.6: Jensen's Alpha by Bollinger Band Length

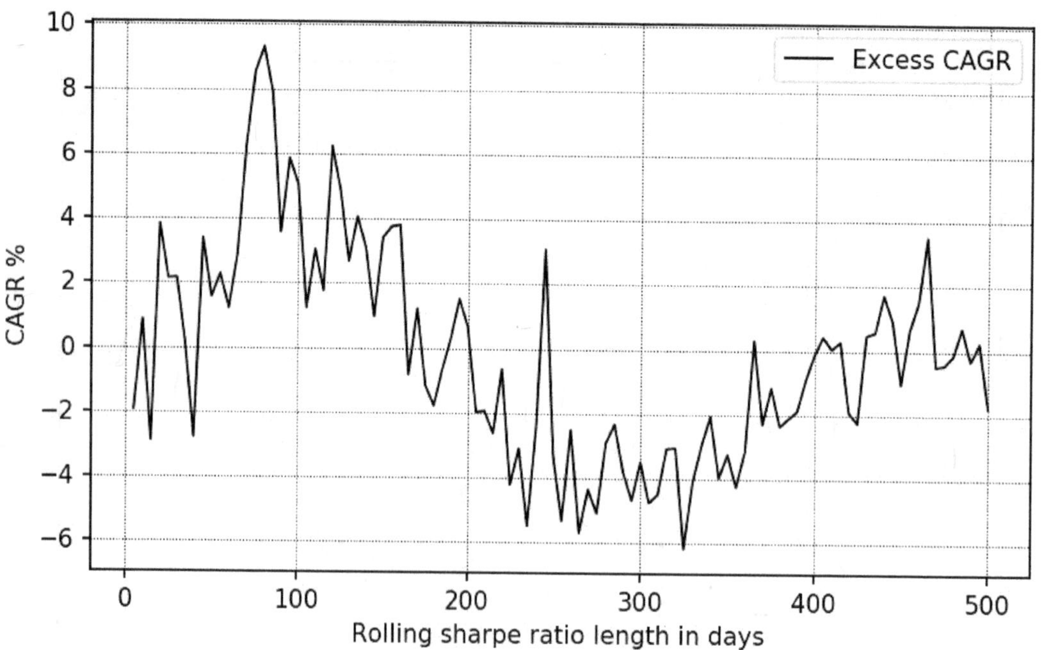

Figure 4.7: Excess CAGR by Rolling Sharpe Ratio Length

performance.

See Figures 4.8 and 4.9 for excess CAGR and Sharpe Ratio by `max_active_positions`.

The behavior of excess CAGR is consistent with our understanding of trading fees. Closer inspection reveals that the equity curve of the portfolio very tightly hugs the S&P 500 when `max_active_positions` is high. These strategies will slightly underperform the broader market because they trade very frequently, incurring numerous trading fees.

The behavior of the Sharpe Ratio is also consistent with our understanding of diversification. When diversification reduces volatility while also providing smaller overall returns than an undiversified alternative, its Sharpe Ratio will stay nearly constant.

4.3.3 Tweaking Trading Costs

The default trading costs in our simulator are \$1 to open a position and 0.05% adverse slippage when opening and closing a position. These are reasonable estimates for most retail brokerages, but the cost and execution performance may differ between brokerages.

It is no surprise what happens to the portfolio performance when we increase the trading costs. See Figure 4.10 and 4.11. Note that our simulator will throw assertion errors if you increase the fees to the point where your strategy does not have enough cash to cover trading fees.

4.4 Simulation Design Principles

One of the most important purposes of this book is to provide readers with the experience necessary to create functional simulators by documenting and discussing one type of simulator. Your simulator might be

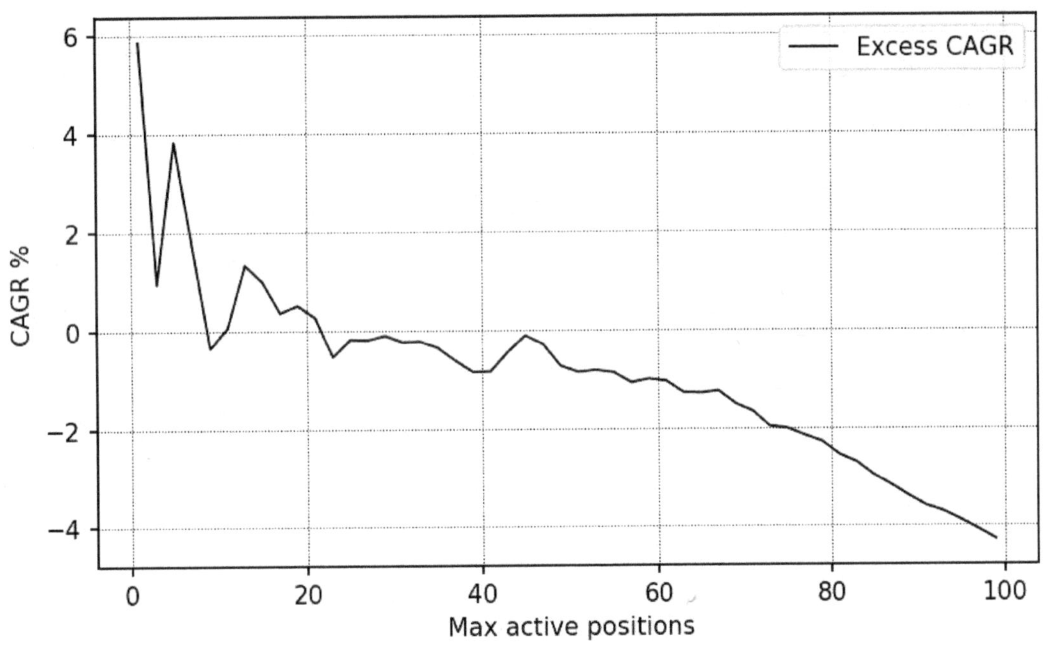

Figure 4.8: Excess CAGR by Max Active Positions

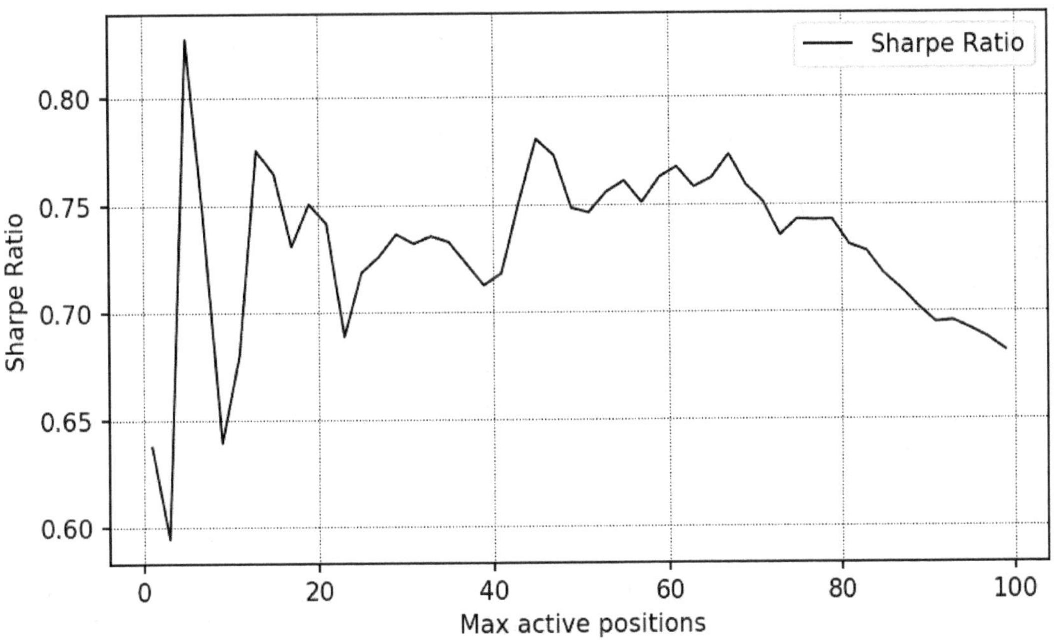

Figure 4.9: Sharpe Ratio by Max Active Positions

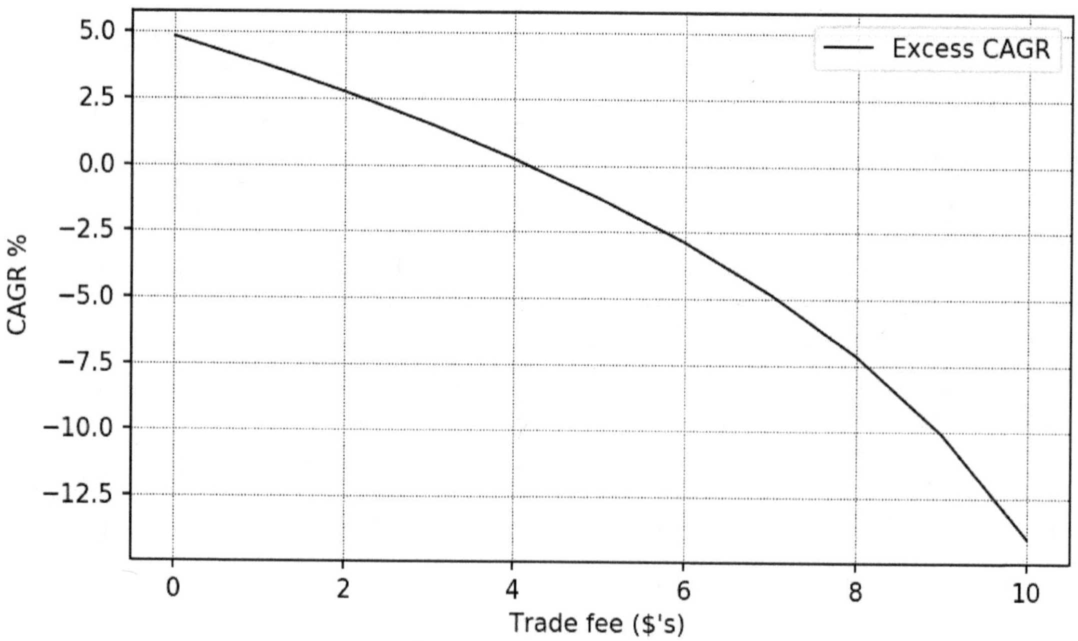

Figure 4.10: Excess CAGR by Trade Fees

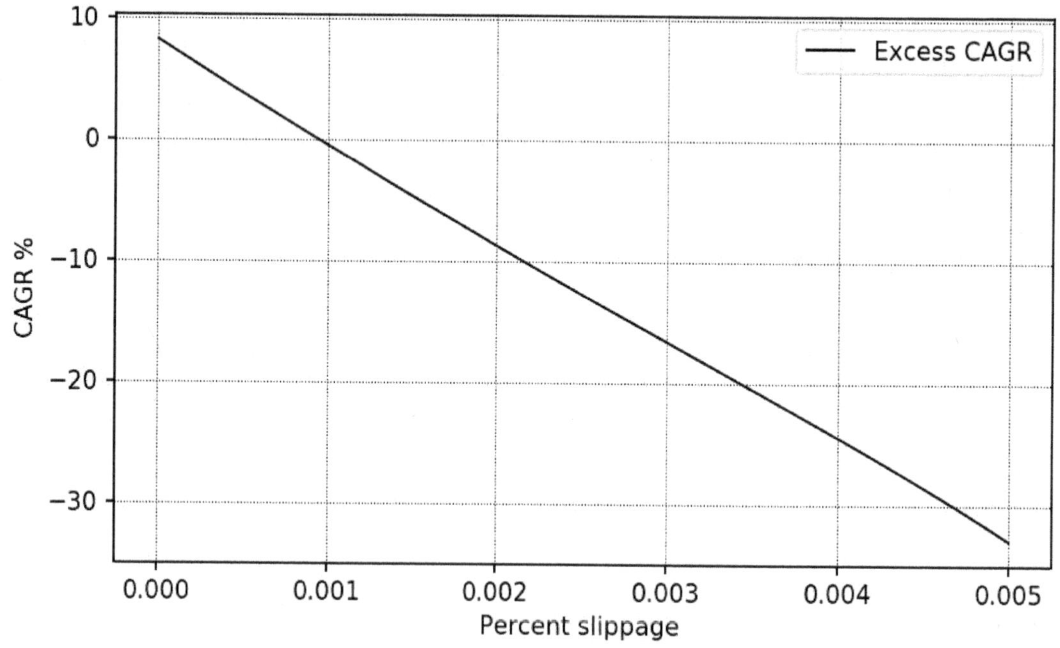

Figure 4.11: Excess CAGR by Percent Slippage

a modification of the one presented here, or it may be something entirely different. The section will discuss important design principles to consider when developing a simulator.

4.4.1 Avoid Generalization

Quantitative strategy developers often see a simulator like the one presented in this chapter and immediately want to start generalizing and extending it to handle other types of strategies and assets. Since this strategy handles long-only multi-asset equity strategies, readers might want to generalize it to simultaneously handle short positions, long and short derivatives, currencies, futures, and real estate, all at once. The purpose of this section is to discourage them from doing that.

Simulators do not easily generalize to handle other asset classes and trade types. They also do not generalize to handle data from different providers or arbitrarily formatted data. In general, one type of trading strategy and one data source should combine to create their own unique simulator. While it is technically possible to create *one simulator to rule them all*, I am making the argument that it would inhibit the speed of innovation to do so.

The simulator we constructed in this chapter is about 400 lines of Python code. I would consider this rather short given the breadth and complexity of the job that it does. It is only 400 lines of code because it makes numerous implicit assumptions about the character of the data and the constraints on the account. In order to extend it, for example, to handle short positions simultaneously, it would need another 400 lines of code that dealt specifically with margin constraints and the resulting impact those have on a hybrid portfolio. Additionally, our officially supported features and behaviors we named earlier in the chapter would multiply in complexity and contain numerous new assumptions about the desired behavior of the portfolio in margin-specific scenarios. Further, our performance metrics would be need to be altered to handle equity curves that can become negative.

Strategy simulation is a research task as opposed to an application development task. When we are doing research, we are not trying to maintain the largest, most feature-complete, and bug-free codebase of simulation logic. Rather, we are trying to develop a lean, well-documented, and understandable subset of relevant simulation logic, such that we can be confident in the outputs from our simulator and always cognizant of its underlying assumptions. Thus, when handling a new type of simulation, write a new simulator. When writing new simulators, feel free to copy and paste relevant pieces of logic where it makes sense, but avoid generalizing.

As a final word on this topic, I have written the following list of generalization pitfalls for simulators. All of the items in this list are things that cannot be always accounted for, predicted uniformly, or generalized away.

- The shape and character of your data.
- The patterns of missing values in your data.
- Data structures of signals and criteria for executing against signals.
- The account requirements of your potential brokerages.
- Account management requirements for the specific asset class.
- The implementation details of trading the asset.
- Which assumptions or conditions are valid and reasonable.

Since there is no *one simulator to rule them all* we will move on to provide guidance on what qualifies a simulator as good.

4.4.2 Criteria for Goodness

There is no strictly correct way to write a simulator. When we think about the quality of simulators, we should not think about them as being either correct or incorrect. Instead, we should think about them as being either good or bad.

The criteria for goodness in a simulator includes financial concepts like replicability, realism, and integration of known trading parameters, but they are also software development concepts like usability, documentation, and simplicity. In other words, a financially valid simulator is only good insofar as it follows the rules of good software design. Following from our discussion about generalization, the following is a list of things you might see in a bad simulator.

- **Unrealistic penalties, commissions, and slippage** If a simulator does not make an effort to mirror the target brokerage's characteristics in this regard, then it is bad. We saw in the above experiments that the CAGR nearly doubles on our example strategy when we eliminate slippage.
- **Unacceptable computational complexity** A simulator should be nearly $O(nm)$ in computational complexity for n rows and m columns of data. If it is difficult to verify on paper, it can be verified in through profiling. Our simulator's runtime is sublinear with $n * m$ according to profiling.
- **Unacceptable assumptions** There is no end to the possibilities on this topic. It is not uncommon to see margin strategies that assume the impossibility of a margin call. I would consider those types of assumptions unacceptable in a good simulation.
- **Data leakage** This term refers to using information in the future to inform past trading decisions. It is easy to accidentally do this in a simulator. For example, if you simulator uses opening prices to buy assets, but derives signals from closing prices on the same date, there is data leakage, and the results are invalid. This problem is more insidious when we deal with machine learning strategies, which we will discuss later in the book.

4.5 Conclusion

In this chapter we have learned how to build a simulator, what characteristics make a good simulator, and how to study basic market dynamics by tweaking our simulator. The next chapter on optimization will take the concept of tweaking to the next level by exploring multivariate relationships between input parameters.

Chapter 5

Optimization

In quantitative trading, optimization is the process of systematically exploring combinations of input parameters to maximize the value of a performance metric. This chapter will not only discuss the code required to run basic optimization routines, but also the proper usage and interpretation of results from optimization studies.

5.1 Background

Optimization has a wide range of meanings in mathematics and science. In this book, we will be looking strictly at numerical optimization. When we work with numerical optimization, as opposed to analytical optimization, we are forgoing nearly all assumptions about the shape of the objective function. The only assumption we will make is that the objective function is real-valued over the prescribed domain.

5.1.1 Optimization in Context

Regardless of what type of optimization we are dealing with, the basic problem of optimization can be described as determining,

$$\underset{\theta}{\operatorname{argmax}}[f(\theta)]$$

where $f(\cdot)$ is our objective function and θ is a vector of parameters. In quantitative trading, the objective function is a performance metric, like a Sharpe Ratio or Jensen's Alpha, and the parameter vector consists of any input parameters affecting the behavior of the simulation. Elements of the parameter vector might include a moving average length or a maximum number of active positions.

In the process of optimization, we will ascertain a few useful things other than the optimal parameter vector. We will also determine an optimization path or optimization surface. These refer to all of the values of the objective function that were evaluated in the process of locating the maxima. Plots and visualizations of these values are often more helpful in the course of research than the optimal parameter vector itself.

5.1.2 Optimization Methods

Many numerical optimization methods exist, and I have documented their application to trading strategies in my previous publications. Some of the most popular numerical optimization methods include Genetic, Nelder-Mead, BFGS, and Pattern Search.

We will be working with what is arguably the simplest numerical optimization method, known as *grid search*. The grid search algorithm takes fixed ranges of parameters as inputs and tests every possible combination of them along an n-dimensional grid.

The grid search algorithm is particularly advantageous to trading simulations for a few reasons.

1. It excels with a small number of parameters.
2. It allows us to evaluate multiple objective functions at the same time.
3. It does not get stuck on local maximas.
4. It can evaluate non-linear and non-continuous ranges of parameters.
5. It creates excellent visualizations.

Most importantly, grid search is ideal for this application because, as strategy developers, we do not actually care about finding the maxima of the objective function. The maxima of any one optimization is necessarily a result of overfitting, and is necessarily a local maxima rather than a global maxima. The parameter vector from a local maxima is not only an overfit, but it will not be the ideal parameter vector in a production trading scenario.

As strategy developers, we care about researching our strategies and visualizing the results of these experiments to develop an intuitive understanding of how our strategies perform in real trading scenarios. For example, if the optimization surface of your strategy contains hundreds of losing configurations, but one exceptional configuration, you are likely to consider that exceptionally performing configuration to be a lark – an overfit that is the result of noise. What you would prefer to see, as a level-headed strategy developer, is a strategy that performs modestly well over a large area of the parameter space, such that you feel confident trading in real life with the parameters of any member of that group.

We will move on to discuss the code for our grid search optimizer.

5.1.3 Goals of Optimization

As mentioned previously, our efforts in optimization are for exploration and understanding. This means that our efforts in optimization are explicitly not intended for trivial acts of curve-fitting. When we run multiple trials of a simulation, we are guaranteed to encounter trials that perform better than others. It is also likely we will encounter outliers that perform much better or much worse than others. It is not our goal to pluck those outliers from the heap of regular performers and advertise them as exceptional trading strategies.

The academic community has lobbed a lot of criticism over the years, both at itself and the larger quant community, over the ways various trading softwares seem to prioritize and encourage curve-fitting. Having used some such software very early in my career, I can say this is a valid criticism.

I feel the need to acknowledge and dispel the notion that I am encouraging any form of curve-fitting through the software I am making available in this book. My distaste for curve-fitting is one of the main reasons this chapter will only focus on grid search optimization, as opposed to other types of optimization. Grid search algorithms yield local maxima, but they also yield important research material. Other optimization algorithms that were designed to locate maxima in high-dimensional parameter spaces typically result in curve-fitting without yielding useful research material.

5.2 Grid Search Algorithm

The grid search algorithm is very simple. Given n parameters, each with a range of values to test, test every single combination of values as an n-dimensional grid. Let n_i denote the number of values in range i. The number of tests would be $n_1 * n_2 * ...$ in total.

A naive Python implementation would look like a series of nested loops. For example, for $n = 4$ parameters, you might have some code like the following.

```
# Psuedo-code for 4-dimensional grid search
for p_one in param_one_range:
    for p_two in param_two_range:
        for p_three in param_three_range:
            for p_four in param_four_range:
                results = simulate(p_one, p_two, p_three, p_four)
                # Do something with the results
```

Thus, the number of times the simulator will run would be equal to `len(param_one_range) * len(param_two_range) ....`

In practice, we will use `itertools.product` to simulate the effect of running n nested loops. The function `product([1,2],['a','b'])` returns an iterator that evaluates to `(1,'a'),(1,'b'),(2,'a'),(2,'b')`. The `GridSearchOptimizer` we will define will be essentially this with additional data organization, summary, timing, and plotting utilities built into it.

5.2.1 Defining the Grid Search Optimizer

The code for the grid search optimizer is as follows.

```
from pypm import metrics, signals, data_io, simulation

import pandas as pd
import numpy as np
from collections import defaultdict, OrderedDict
from itertools import product
from timeit import default_timer
from typing import Dict, Tuple, List, Callable, Iterable, Any, NewType, Mapping

import matplotlib.pyplot as plt
from matplotlib import cm
from mpl_toolkits.mplot3d import Axes3D

# Performance data and parameter inputs are dictionaries
Parameters = NewType('Parameters', Dict[str, float])
Performance = simulation.PortfolioHistory.PerformancePayload # Dict[str, float]

# Simulation function must take parameters as keyword arguments pointing to
# iterables and return a performance metric dictionary
SimKwargs = NewType('Kwargs', Mapping[str, Iterable[Any]])
SimFunction = NewType('SimFunction', Callable[[SimKwargs], Performance])

class OptimizationResult(object):
    """Simple container class for optimization data"""

    def __init__(self, parameters: Parameters, performance: Performance):

        # Make sure no collisions between performance metrics and params
        assert len(parameters.keys() & performance.keys()) == 0, \
            'parameter name matches performance metric name'

        self.parameters = parameters
        self.performance = performance

    @property
```

```
    def as_dict(self) -> Dict[str, float]:
        """Combines the dictionaries after we are sure of no collisions"""
        return {**self.parameters, **self.performance}


class GridSearchOptimizer(object):
    """
    A generic grid search optimizer that requires only a simulation function and
    a series of parameter ranges. Provides timing, summary, and plotting
    utilities with return data.
    """

    def __init__(self, simulation_function: SimFunction):

        self.simulate = simulation_function
        self._results_list: List[OptimizationResult] = list()
        self._results_df = pd.DataFrame()

        self._optimization_finished = False

    def add_results(self, parameters: Parameters, performance: Performance):
        _results = OptimizationResult(parameters, performance)
        self._results_list.append(_results)

    def optimize(self, **optimization_ranges: SimKwargs):

        assert optimization_ranges, 'Must provide non-empty parameters.'

        # Convert all iterables to lists
        param_ranges = {k: list(v) for k, v in optimization_ranges.items()}
        self.param_names = param_names = list(param_ranges.keys())

        # Count total simulation
        n = total_simulations = np.prod([len(r) for r in param_ranges.values()])

        total_time_elapsed = 0

        print(f'Starting simulation ...')
        print(f'Simulating 1 / {n} ...', end='\r')
        for i, params in enumerate(product(*param_ranges.values())):
            if i > 0:
                _avg = avg_time = total_time_elapsed / i
                _rem = remaining_time = (n - (i + 1)) * avg_time
                s =  f'Simulating {i+1} / {n} ... '
                s += f'{_rem:.0f}s remaining ({_avg:.1f}s avg)'
                s += ' '*8
                print(s, end='\r')

            timer_start = default_timer()

            parameters = {n: param for n, param in zip(param_names, params)}
            results = self.simulate(**parameters)
            self.add_results(parameters, results)
```

```
            timer_end = default_timer()
            total_time_elapsed += timer_end - timer_start

        print(f'Simulated {total_simulations} / {total_simulations} ...')
        print(f'Elapsed time: {total_time_elapsed:.0f}s')
        print(f'Done.')

        self._optimization_finished = True

    def _assert_finished(self):
        assert self._optimization_finished, \
            'Run self.optimize before accessing this method.'

    @property
    def results(self) -> pd.DataFrame:
        self._assert_finished()
        if self._results_df.empty:

            _results_list = self._results_list
            self._results_df = pd.DataFrame([r.as_dict for r in _results_list])

            _columns = set(list(self._results_df.columns.values))
            _params = set(self.param_names)
            self.metric_names = list(_columns - _params)

        return self._results_df

    def print_summary(self):
        df = self.results
        metric_names = self.metric_names

        print('Summary statistics')
        print(df[metric_names].describe().T)

    def get_best(self, metric_name: str) -> pd.DataFrame:
        """
        Sort the results by a specific performance metric
        """
        self._assert_finished()

        results = self.results
        param_names = self.param_names
        metric_names = self.metric_names

        assert metric_name in metric_names, 'Not a performance metric'
        partial_df = self.results[param_names+[metric_name]]

        return partial_df.sort_values(metric_name, ascending=False)

    def plot_1d_hist(self, x, show=True):
        self.results.hist(x)
        if show:
            plt.show()
```

```
def plot_2d_line(self, x, y, show=True, **filter_kwargs):
    _results = self.results
    for k, v in filter_kwargs.items():
        _results = _results[getattr(_results, k) == v]

    ax = _results.plot(x, y)
    if filter_kwargs:
        k_str = ', '.join([f'{k}={v}' for k,v in filter_kwargs.items()])
        ax.legend([f'{x} ({k_str})'])

    if show:
        plt.show()

def plot_2d_violin(self, x, y, show=True):
    """
    Group y along x then plot violin charts
    """
    x_values = self.results[x].unique()
    x_values.sort()

    y_by_x = OrderedDict([(v, []) for v in x_values])
    for _, row in self.results.iterrows():
        y_by_x[row[x]].append(row[y])

    fig, ax = plt.subplots()

    ax.violinplot(dataset=list(y_by_x.values()), showmedians=True)
    ax.set_xlabel(x)
    ax.set_ylabel(y)
    ax.set_xticks(range(0, len(y_by_x)+1))
    ax.set_xticklabels([''] + list(y_by_x.keys()))
    if show:
        plt.show()

def plot_3d_mesh(self, x, y, z, show=True, **filter_kwargs):
    """
    Plot interactive 3d mesh. z axis should typically be performance metric
    """
    _results = self.results
    fig = plt.figure()
    ax = Axes3D(fig)

    for k, v in filter_kwargs.items():
        _results = _results[getattr(_results, k) == v]

    X, Y, Z = [getattr(_results, attr) for attr in (x, y, z)]
    ax.plot_trisurf(X, Y, Z, cmap=cm.jet, linewidth=0.2)
    ax.set_xlabel(x)
    ax.set_ylabel(y)
    ax.set_zlabel(z)
    if show:
        plt.show()

def plot(self, *attrs: Tuple[str], show=True,
```

```
        **filter_kwargs: Dict[str, Any]):
    """
    Attempt to intelligently dispatch plotting functions based on the number
    and type of attributes. Last argument should typically be the
    performance metric.
    """
    self._assert_finished()
    param_names = self.param_names
    metric_names = self.metric_names

    if len(attrs) == 3:
        assert attrs[0] in param_names and attrs[1] in param_names, \
            'First two positional arguments must be parameter names.'

        assert attrs[2] in metric_names, \
            'Last positional argument must be a metric name.'

        assert len(filter_kwargs) + 2 == len(param_names), \
            'Must filter remaining parameters. e.g. p_three=some_number.'

        self.plot_3d_mesh(*attrs, show=show, **filter_kwargs)

    elif len(attrs) == 2:
        if len(param_names) == 1 or filter_kwargs:
            self.plot_2d_line(*attrs, show=show, **filter_kwargs)

        elif len(param_names) > 1:
            self.plot_2d_violin(*attrs, show=show)

    elif len(attrs) == 1:
        self.plot_1d_hist(*attrs, show=show)

    else:
        raise ValueError('Must pass between one and three column names.')
```

Listing 5.1: Grid search optimizer

Notice the `GridSearchOptimizer.optimize` method. The core of that logic is essentially the pseudo-code at the beginning of the chapter. We loop through the output of `itertools.product` and store all of the results for later analysis.

Note how the input to the `__init__` function of the optimizer is a simulation function. Investigating the type hints, we can see that this function should accept only keyword arguments pointing to iterables and returns a dictionary of performance metrics. In the context of our previous examples, these keyword arguments will be things like `bollinger_n=[5, 10, 20, 40, ...]` or `sharpe_n=range(20, 120, 20)` to indicate we want to explore those parameters over those ranges of values. Since the simulation function accepts *only* parameters with optimization ranges, we must *bind* the rest of the relevant data directly to the simulation function. Binding the static data will have the dual effect of standardizing the input parameters for the optimizer and preventing unnecessary duplicate operations.

Recall the discussion in the previous chapter about classes as interfaces and good software design principles. We have built the optimizer in this way, however complicated it may seem, because the result is a relatively clean interface for researching trading strategies. Readers do not need to fully understand the Python mechanics of this class to benefit from it. Simply follow along with these examples.

5.2.2 Using the Grid Search Optimizer

See Listing 5.2 for an example using the grid search optimizer. The work here is in binding the data to the simulation function. Notice the function **bind_simulator** builds and returns a function, which becomes the **simulation_function** argument to the optimizer. This is a classic design pattern for generic optimizers in computer science, but it means that defining the optimizer is only half the battle.

As mentioned previously, binding the data to the simulation function has a lot of advantages. Notice how all of the calls to **data_io** are done outside the **_simulate** definition, and those pieces of data are bound to the **_simulate** function. Internally, Python is storing a reference to the **prices** data frame and giving the **_simulate** function access to it without requiring it to be an argument. This means that we only need to load the data in once, which saves a lot of time (a little over a second) on each call to the simulator. Further, we have mentioned previously how we will be wrangling with machine learning and alternative data later in this book. This design pattern needs no modifications to handle those methods, because the optimizer itself does not need to know anything about the simulator, signals, or the input data to work.

```
import pandas as pd

from pypm import metrics, signals, data_io, simulation, optimization
from pypm.optimization import GridSearchOptimizer

from typing import List, Dict, Tuple, Callable

Performance = simulation.PortfolioHistory.PerformancePayload # Dict[str, float]

def bind_simulator(**sim_kwargs) -> Callable:
    """
    Create a function with all static simulation data bound to it, where the
    arguments are simulation parameters
    """

    symbols: List[str] = data_io.get_all_symbols()
    prices: pd.DataFrame = data_io.load_eod_matrix(symbols)

    _bollinger: Callable = signals.create_bollinger_band_signal
    _sharpe: Callable = metrics.calculate_rolling_sharpe_ratio

    def _simulate(bollinger_n: int, sharpe_n: int) -> Performance:

        signal = prices.apply(_bollinger, args=(bollinger_n,), axis=0)
        preference = prices.apply(_sharpe, args=(sharpe_n, ), axis=0)

        simulator = simulation.SimpleSimulator(**sim_kwargs)
        simulator.simulate(prices, signal, preference)

        return simulator.portfolio_history.get_performance_metric_data()

    return _simulate

if __name__ == '__main__':

    simulate = bind_simulator(initial_cash=10000, max_active_positions=5)

    optimizer = GridSearchOptimizer(simulate)
    optimizer.optimize(
```

```
        bollinger_n=range(10, 110, 10),
        sharpe_n=range(10, 110, 10),
    )

    print(optimizer.get_best('excess_cagr'))
    optimizer.plot('excess_cagr')
    optimizer.plot('bollinger_n', 'excess_cagr')
    optimizer.plot('bollinger_n', 'sharpe_n', 'excess_cagr')

# Returns ...
#      bollinger_n  sharpe_n  excess_cagr
# 17            20        80     0.092841
# 16            20        70     0.062477
# 98           100        90     0.055047
# 19            20       100     0.050255
# 1             10        20     0.043642
# ..           ...       ...          ...
# 89            90       100    -0.054080
# 69            70       100    -0.054404
# 63            70        40    -0.061105
# 61            70        20    -0.063276
# 50            60        10    -0.065433
```

Listing 5.2: Grid search optimizer example

Figures 5.1, 5.2, and 5.3 show various plots for this optimization. There is a lot of potentially valuable exploratory analysis readers can do with this bit of code. The best way to do this analysis is to run the script in `ipython` or Jupyter Notebooks in interactive mode. For example, running `ipython -i optimize_portfolio.py` will run the optimization then let you play with the plotting and summary functions by calling things like `optimizer.plot('bollinger_n', 'jensens_alpha')`.

These results are open to interpretation. As mentioned previously, optimization and simulation in this context are not well-defined statistical tests with binary outcomes. It can even be argued that part of the intuitive understanding we seek to develop is entirely non-verbal. Nonetheless, my impressions from these figures are as follows.

The histogram of excess CAGR in Figure 5.1 is fairly symmetrical about 0, and the mean excess CAGR is a small negative number. This suggests that the Bollinger Band indicator and the signal we are deriving from it, in general, are not uncovering new information about market movements. We will seek to quantify this idea more thoroughly later in the chapter.

According to Figures 5.2 and 5.3, the Bollinger Band and Rolling Sharpe Ratio work better for smaller values of `bollinger_n` and higher values of `sharpe_n`. There is potentially more positive territory to explore for even higher values of `bollinger_n` and `sharpe_n`, if we extrapolate the shape of the 3D mesh in Figure 5.3.

If you are stress-testing a potentially revolutionary strategy, these charts would generally *not* be what you want to see. These charts exhibit small clusters of excellent performance and large clusters of poor performance for reasonable parameter values. Further, these charts do not provide any evidence of consistent outperformance due to the intrinsic value of the underlying indicators. If this strategy did provide intrinsically market-beating information, the mean excess CAGR across this set of parameters would not be negative or near-zero, and the distribution of excess CAGR would not be nearly symmetric about zero.

There is a lot of joking and folklore in the trading community about some traders that are so bad that you can make money by reversing their trading decisions. Keep this in mind as you are exploring strategies. A distribution like Figure 5.1 that is nearly symmetric about zero is much less interesting than a distribution that is profoundly negative. By adjusting our signals appropriately, a significantly negative distribution can become a significantly positive one. Also, keep in mind that trading costs and slippage provide a small but

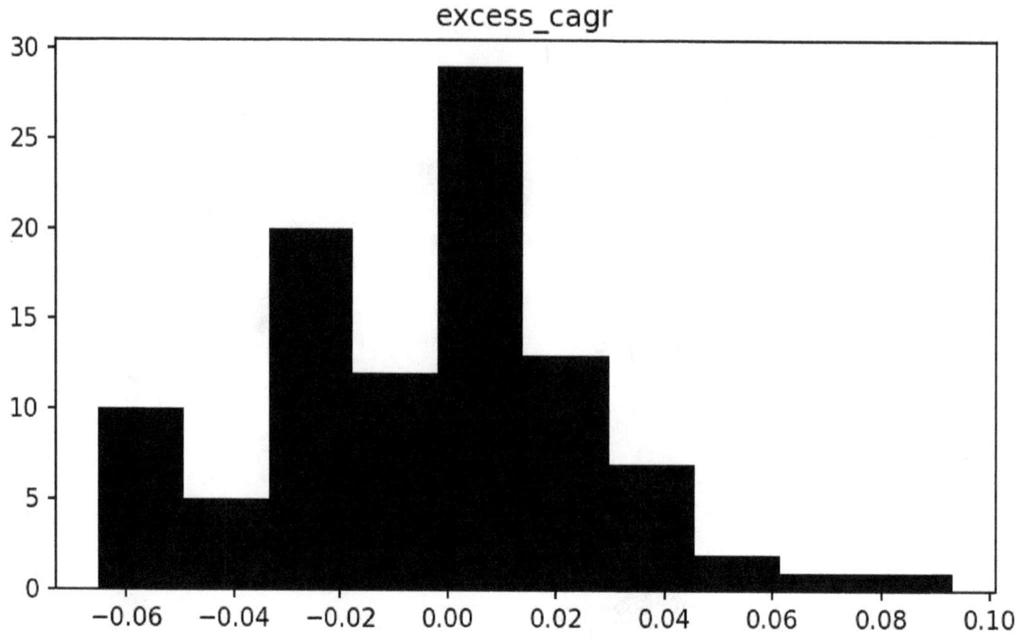

Figure 5.1: Histogram of Excess CAGR for Optimization

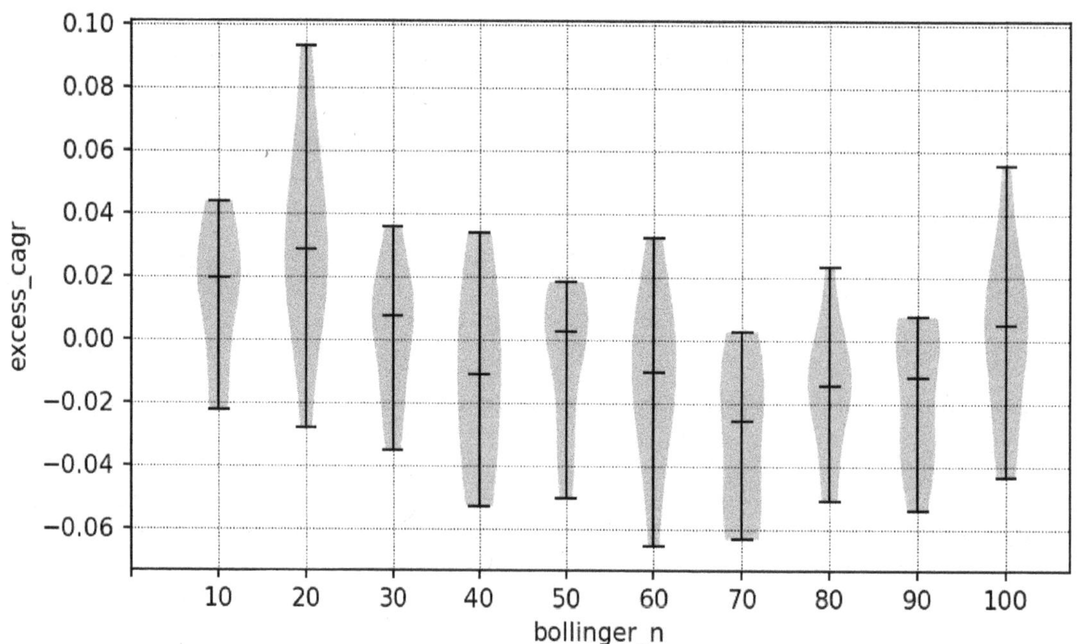

Figure 5.2: Excess CAGR by Bollinger Band Length for Optimization

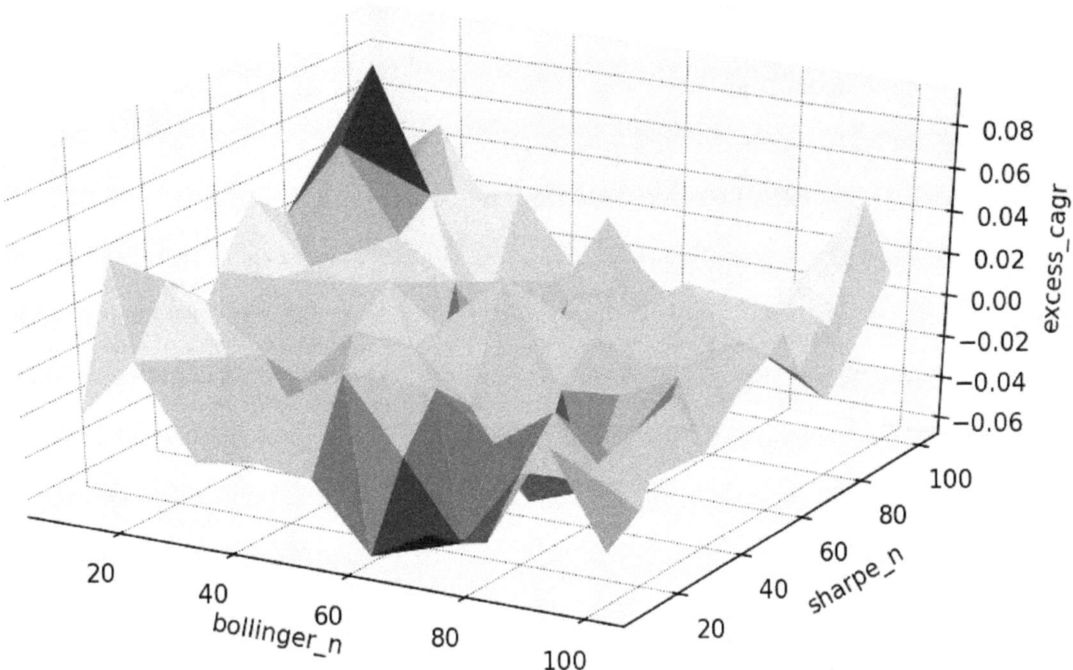

Figure 5.3: Excess CAGR by Bollinger Band and Rolling Sharpe Length

significant constant negative drag on our returns. So, when we are fighting to beat the S&P 500 on excess CAGR, we are simultaneously trying to compensate for fees we incur from frequent trading.

Readers are encouraged to experiment with the grid search optimizer by modifying the signals, preference matrix, parameters, and input data to research new strategies. Unlike our `SimpleSimulator` from the last chapter that only handles long-only multi-asset strategies, the `GridSearchOptimizer` is a pretty generic implementation that can be used for nearly any type of trading strategy. Ultimately, the grid search optimizer we built does not know anything about the portfolio objects or simulation objects we built in the last chapter. It only knows it explores multiple ranges of parameters.

Readers might notice that the optimizer can take a long time to run. My machine is averaging about 2 seconds per iteration, meaning an 1,800 item grid search would take an hour. See the following pieces of advice to deal with computation time.

- You likely never need to run a 1,000+ item search. If you do, you are likely attempting to overfit a strategy. It is a tenant of non-parametric statistics that statistical power in numerical simulations achieves very marginal improvements above 1,000 simulations. This tenant even applies to simulations that take fractions of a millisecond per iteration.
- You are free to attempt to parallelize the grid search optimizer. I would not recommend it, though. Instead I would recommend the following.
- You can get full use out of your n-core computer by running n simulations at the same time in different Python processes. This is as simple as opening n terminals and modifying the optimization script before each run. This is why I recommend multiple processes over parallelization. It is generally more useful to test different types of signals than to test massive ranges of parameters.
- Always terminate your script in an interactive terminal with `python -i some_script.py` or `ipython -i some_script.py`. This will allow you to explore relationships between your parameters freely after the optimization completes.

- Store the results of your optimization to a CSV file using `optimizer.results.to_csv('some_file.csv')`. You can load it into memory later to analyze it. Though, you will lose access to the utilities in `GridSearchOptimizer`.

We will move on to discuss some more applications of the grid search optimizer.

5.3 Non-parametric Methods

The term *non-parametric statistics* refers to a field of study within statistics where statistical tests make no assumptions about the underlying shape of the probability distribution of the random variable. In classical statistics, the term *parametric* refers to how statistical tests are *parameterized* via assumed probability distributions. Non-parametric statistics as a field makes heavy use of permutation, simulation, ranking, scoring, and bootstrapping. This field has laid the foundation for the development of many popular non-parametric models we use in modern machine learning.

This section is not about non-parametric statistics in the sense that it will not define formal testing methodologies or write out hypothesis tests, but it will draw inspiration from non-parametric methods to develop some novel tests for our trading strategy. Using the `GridSearchOptimizer` as our framework, we will modify the simulation function in a number of ways to learn about the underlying mechanics of our strategy.

Our language in this section might become confusing at times, because we will be running trading simulations on simulated data. The word *simulation* will be thrown around a lot with different meanings depending on the context.

5.3.1 White Noise Test

Earlier in this chapter, we plotted a histogram of excess CAGR over a grid of different parameter values and found that it was nearly symmetric about its mean of nearly zero. Interpreting this result, I mentioned that this was good evidence that the Bollinger Band and Rolling Sharpe Ratio strategy was not generally providing market-beating information. Nonetheless, there were pockets of values in the 3D plot that performed particularly well.

When we say a pocket of values performs *particularly well*, how can we tell if that magnitude of performance was the result of random noise? In this section, we will provide white noise as inputs to various parts of our strategy in order to get a better idea for how the market responds nearly random decision-making. Comparing the performance of our strategy to nearly random decisions will help us determine if our stock picks are better than those of the proverbial monkey throwing darts.

We will start by providing white noise to our preference matrix. While writing this book and using the Bollinger Band and Rolling Sharpe Ratio example strategy, I have developed a suspicion that the Rolling Sharpe Ratio does not actually provide any value to the strategy. See Listing 5.3 for a test of this theory.

```
import pandas as pd
import numpy as np

from pypm import metrics, signals, data_io, simulation, optimization
from pypm.optimization import GridSearchOptimizer

from typing import List, Dict, Tuple, Callable

Performance = simulation.PortfolioHistory.PerformancePayload # Dict[str, float]

def bind_simulator(**sim_kwargs) -> Callable:
    """
```

```
    Create a simulator that uses white noise for the preference matrix
    """
    symbols: List[str] = data_io.get_all_symbols()
    prices: pd.DataFrame = data_io.load_eod_matrix(symbols)

    _bollinger: Callable = signals.create_bollinger_band_signal

    # Bollinger n is constant throughout
    bollinger_n = 20

    def _simulate(white_noise_test_id: int) -> Performance:

        signal = prices.apply(_bollinger, args=(bollinger_n,), axis=0)

        # Build a pile of noise in the same shape as the price data
        _noise = np.random.normal(loc=0, scale=1, size=prices.shape)
        _cols = prices.columns
        _index = prices.index
        preference = pd.DataFrame(_noise, columns=_cols, index=_index)

        simulator = simulation.SimpleSimulator(**sim_kwargs)
        simulator.simulate(prices, signal, preference)

        return simulator.portfolio_history.get_performance_metric_data()

    return _simulate

if __name__ == '__main__':

    simulate = bind_simulator(initial_cash=10000, max_active_positions=5)

    optimizer = GridSearchOptimizer(simulate)
    optimizer.optimize(white_noise_test_id=range(1000))

    print(optimizer.get_best('excess_cagr'))
    optimizer.print_summary()
    optimizer.plot('excess_cagr')
```

Listing 5.3: White noise preference matrix

Notice how we have modified the optimization to study white noise. Instead of passing a range of parameters into the optimizer, we pass `range(1000)` as a dummy parameter to indicate that we want to run 1000 simulations. This will make some of 2D and 3D plotting utilities fairly useless, because they depend on surfaces having a distinguishable shape, so we will ignore those plots for now.

In order to establish some idea as to whether the Rolling Sharpe Ratio produces a better preference matrix than white noise, we will select an un-optimized default result from one of our previous tests. The default parameters for this strategy are typically `bollinger_n=20` and `sharpe_n=20`, so we will use the excess CAGR of 3.8% as our basis of comparison for this white noise simulation.

See Figures 5.4 and 5.5 for distributions of excess CAGR. The results run counter to my suspicions. The mean excess CAGR over the simulations is -3.76%, which is nowhere near zero, and the baseline excess CAGR of +3.8% from our previous study is greater than 99.5% percent of the simulated values. The maximum excess CAGR in the simulated data is +5.7%, indicating that it is still possible to outperform the baseline result with random noise.

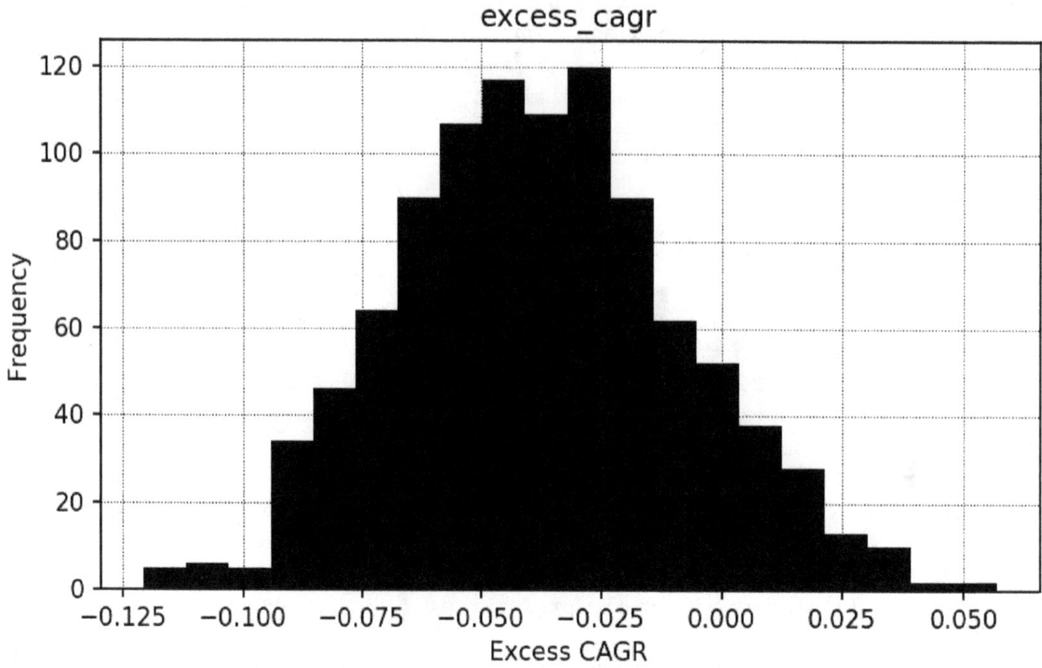

Figure 5.4: Excess CAGR for 1000 White Noise Simulations

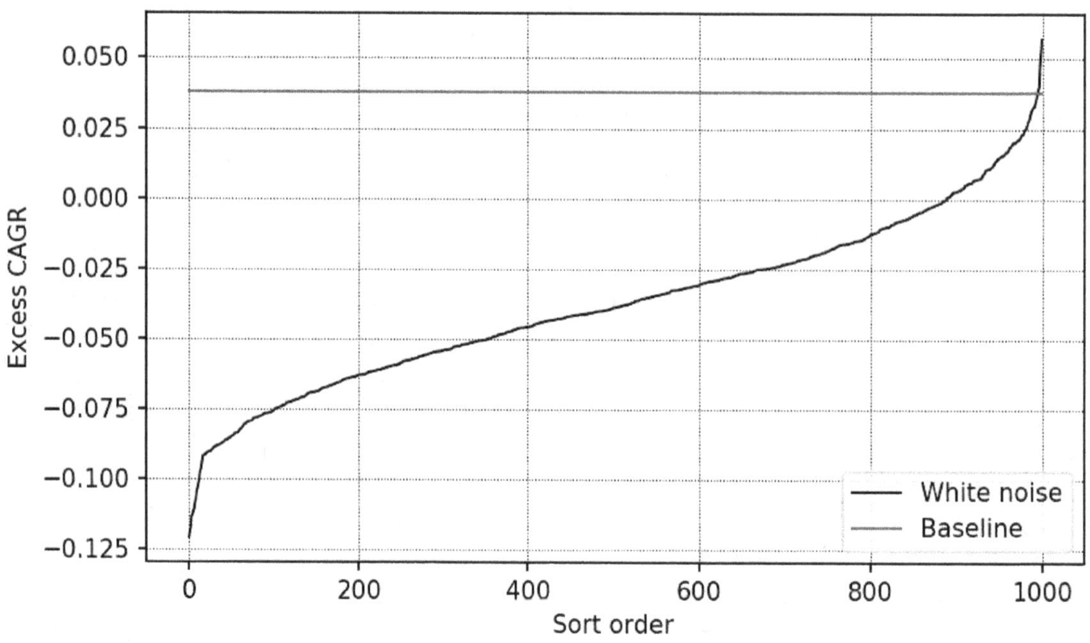

Figure 5.5: Excess CAGR for 1000 White Noise Simulations Sorted

The Rolling Sharpe Ratio likely outperforms random noise in this data because it is a momentum-based indicator. Our simulated data from 2010 through the end of 2019 covers a very long bull market, meaning that momentum-based strategies should outperforms reversal-based strategies in general. Nonetheless, the results from this test are very clean and straightforward. The Rolling Sharpe Ratio clearly helps our strategy performance for `bollinger_n=20`.

Readers may notice the way we constructed and discussed this test feels and sounds very similar to a classical statistical test. As mentioned previously, this research is taking a lot of inspiration from methods in non-parametric statistics. Due to the exploratory nature of this book, we are stopping short discussing null hypotheses, p-values, and significance tests. For example, if we were running rigorous statistical tests, doing a grid search optimization *before* running a white noise simulation would be a flagrant act of p-hacking and data snooping. Instead of running rigorous statistical tests, we are focusing on methodology and implementation.

At this point, astute readers may argue that there is little value in a test that pits an indicator like the Rolling Sharpe Ratio against white noise. After all, white noise has no concept of time, has totally independent observations, and has uniform volatility, all unlike the Rolling Sharpe Ratio. This argument is entirely valid and has been made in many different forms for many different reasons. The class of solutions to this problem is known as bootstrapping, which we will discuss in the next section.

5.3.2 Bootstrap Test

A bootstrap test, or the process of *bootstrapping*, refers to any method that randomly resamples the values of a data set in order run simulations. Instead of generating random values from a normal distribution, bootstrap tests sample values from the input data set. Within the field of non-parametric statistics, bootstrapping is unique because it allows for resampling with replacement, meaning that the same data point can appear in the simulated data set multiple times.

The process of bootstrapping itself does not tell us exactly how we will simulate our data or apply its principles to financial time series. Bootstrapping only tells us that we will be running simulations by sampling with replacement. It is up to us as researchers to decide how those resampled values will create a simulation against which to compare our baseline.

This section will attempt to use bootstrapping to make a fundamental improvement on the white noise test of the previous section. A better simulation test is one where the simulated inputs are closer in character to the original inputs while still being entirely random. We mentioned in the analysis of the white noise test that the Rolling Sharpe Ratio does not have independent observations across time and has non-uniform volatility across time. Our goal in developing a good bootstrapping test will be to develop a randomly simulated preference matrix that has the shape and character of the Rolling Sharpe Ratio preference matrix. Once we do that, we will be able to run a new simulation test. This simulation test will not tell us if the Rolling Sharpe Ratio outperforms random noise, rather, it will tell us if the Rolling Sharpe Ratio outperforms similar randomly generated indicators.

As with some other topics we have discussed so far in this book, there is no exactly correct way to run a bootstrap simulation. There are many valid ways to simulate this data using the source data as the reference distribution. It will be up to us as researchers to use our creativity to develop a method of simulating the Rolling Sharpe Ratio that is both efficient and realistic.

See Listing 5.4 for the approach we settled on. Note the `bootstrap_rolling_sharpe_ratio` function. Since our implementation of the Rolling Sharpe Ratio depends only on the return series as input, we perform bootstrap resampling on the return series of each symbol before calculating the Rolling Sharpe Ratio on it. Thus, we are not simulating the indicator directly, rather, we are simulating the input data for the indicator. Note that we are not modifying the price data or the return series within the actual simulator. We are only created a resampled copy of the return series for use in calculating the indicator.

```
import pandas as pd
import numpy as np
```

```
from pypm import metrics, signals, data_io, simulation, optimization
from pypm.optimization import GridSearchOptimizer

from typing import List, Dict, Tuple, Callable

Performance = simulation.PortfolioHistory.PerformancePayload # Dict[str, float]

def bind_simulator(**sim_kwargs) -> Callable:
    """
    Create a simulator that uses white noise for the preference matrix
    """
    symbols: List[str] = data_io.get_all_symbols()
    prices: pd.DataFrame = data_io.load_eod_matrix(symbols)

    _bollinger: Callable = signals.create_bollinger_band_signal
    bollinger_n = 20

    returns = metrics.calculate_return_series(prices)
    sharpe_n = 20

    def bootstrap_rolling_sharpe_ratio(return_series: pd.Series) -> pd.Series:
        _series = return_series.iloc[1:]
        _series = _series.sample(n=return_series.shape[0], replace=True)
        _series.iloc[:1] = [np.nan]
        _series = pd.Series(_series.values, index=return_series.index)
        _windowed_series = _series.rolling(sharpe_n)
        return _windowed_series.mean() / _windowed_series.std()

    _sharpe: Callable = bootstrap_rolling_sharpe_ratio

    def _simulate(bootstrap_test_id: int) -> Performance:

        signal = prices.apply(_bollinger, args=(bollinger_n,), axis=0)
        preference = returns.apply(_sharpe, axis=0)

        simulator = simulation.SimpleSimulator(**sim_kwargs)
        simulator.simulate(prices, signal, preference)

        return simulator.portfolio_history.get_performance_metric_data()

    return _simulate

if __name__ == '__main__':

    simulate = bind_simulator(initial_cash=10000, max_active_positions=5)

    optimizer = GridSearchOptimizer(simulate)
    optimizer.optimize(bootstrap_test_id=range(1000))

    print(optimizer.get_best('excess_cagr'))
    optimizer.print_summary()
    optimizer.plot('excess_cagr')
```

Listing 5.4: Bootstrap simulated preference matrix

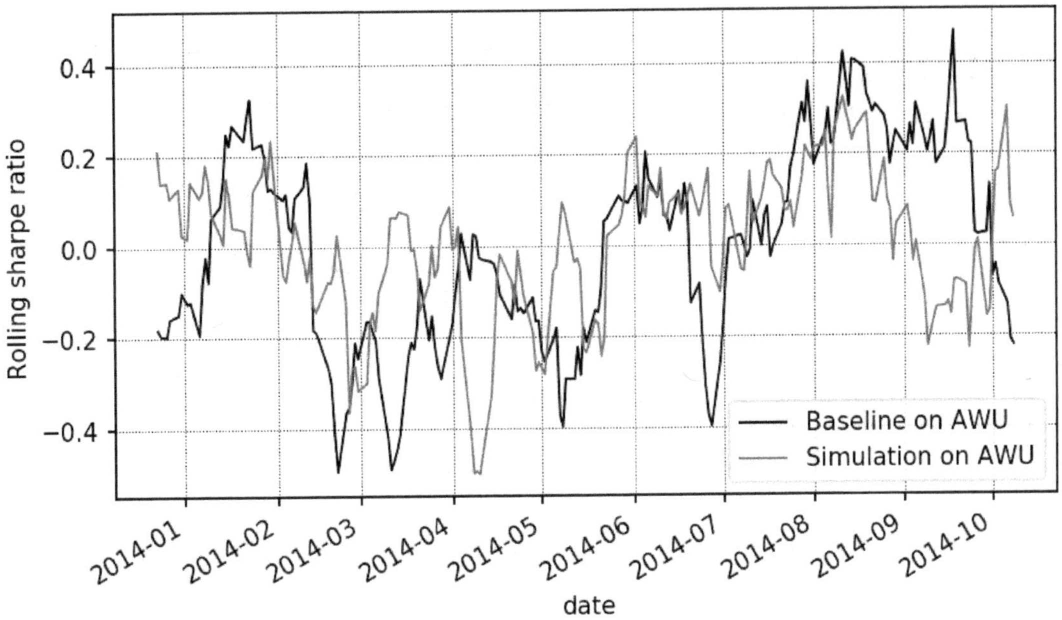

Figure 5.6: Rolling Sharpe Ratio Simulations Comparison

See Figures 5.6 and 5.7 for visualizations of the similarity between the simulated and real Rolling Sharpe Ratio for AWU. See the following terminal output for summary statistics of the real version against the simulated version. Upon visual inspection, the simulated output looks and feels like the real thing, so we will consider it an acceptable bootstrap simulation.

```
#         Simulated AWU     Real AWU  Simulated BMG     Real BMG
# count     2496.000000  2496.000000    2496.000000  2496.000000
# mean         0.069608     0.031267       0.082144     0.052698
# std          0.258862     0.244386       0.229464     0.230124
# min         -0.636159    -0.719587      -0.586900    -0.547204
# 25%         -0.106518    -0.143548      -0.081528    -0.100211
# 50%          0.054543     0.031857       0.077306     0.027837
# 75%          0.235834     0.215793       0.235223     0.195642
# max          1.121245     0.760129       0.859906     1.132237
```

Now that we have verified our bootstrap simulation is realistic enough, we can start running simulations and compare the results to our white noise test. See Figures 5.8 and 5.9 for the results of our simulation.

The bootstrap simulation presented here is much more pessimistic that than the white noise simulation. The mean excess CAGR was 0.9% with a standard deviation of 3.2% compared to a baseline of 3.8%. The baseline outperformed 81% of simulations. In other words, the baseline result was within one standard deviation of the mean, which does not inspire confidence about the value of the trading strategy.

Note that the distribution of performance in Figure 5.8 is symmetric about the mean of nearly zero. When comparing this to the white noise test, it suggests that any preference indicator with at least some smoothness and memory is capable of matching the performance of the overall market on average.

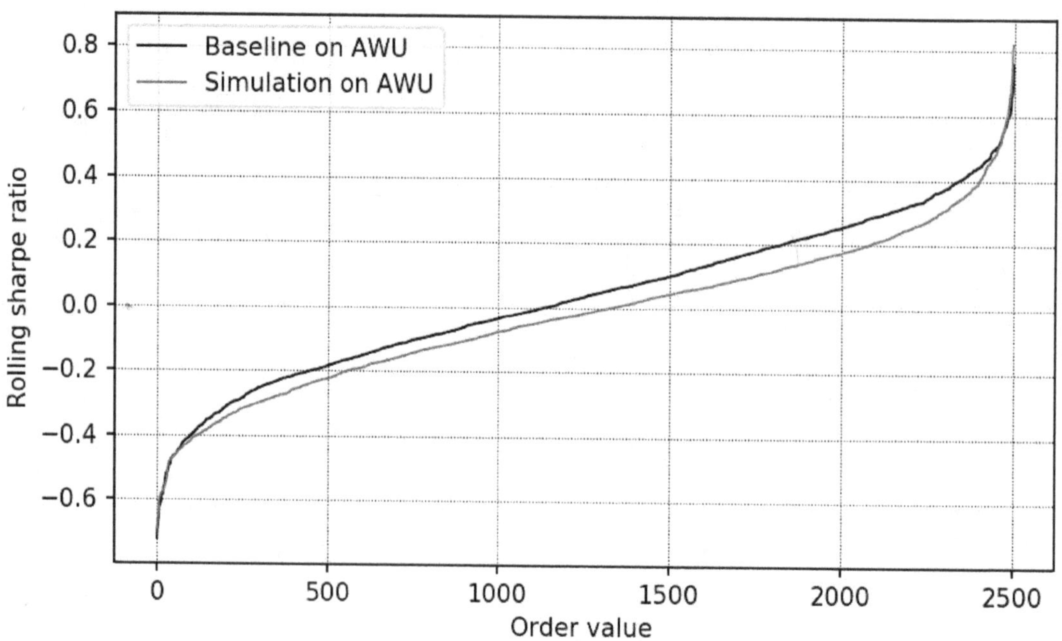

Figure 5.7: Rolling Sharpe Ratio Simulations Distribution Comparison

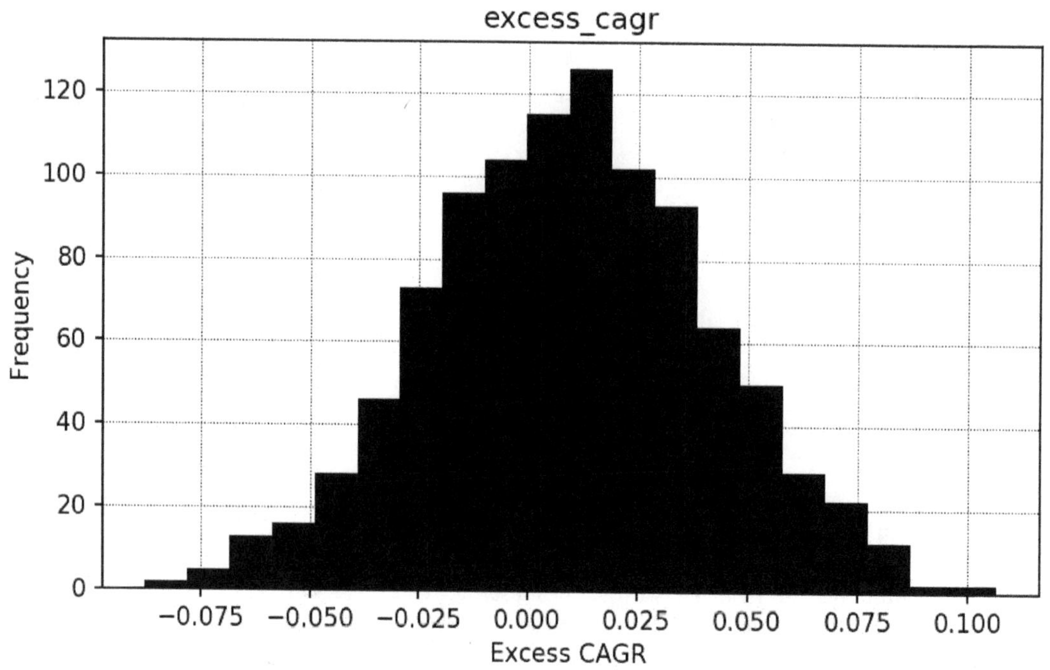

Figure 5.8: Excess CAGR for 1000 Bootstrap Simulations

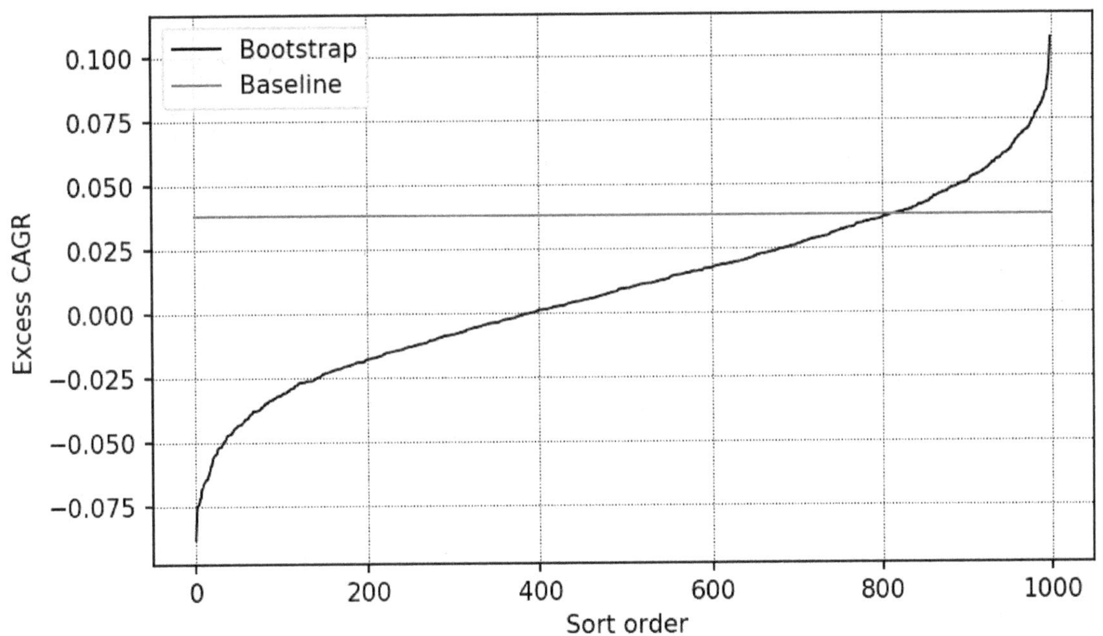

Figure 5.9: Excess CAGR for 1000 Bootstrap Simulations Sorted

5.4 Conclusion

At this point readers may be feeling a bit pessimistic about the prospect of developing a winning trading strategy. So far in this book, we have proposed a system for building multi-asset portfolio strategies, proposed some sample strategies that looked promising, and then cut them down in cold blood using increasingly refined non-parametric tests.

I have not mentioned Jensen's Alpha much in this chapter, because I wanted to keep things interesting. Re-running all of the simulations and tests in this chapter and studying Jensen's Alpha would never reveal a value that is significantly non-zero. In the thousands of simulations we ran in this chapter, and the tens of thousands of simulations I ran in developing and testing this software, no portfolio using the Bollinger Band and Rolling Sharpe Ratio strategy generated a Jensen's Alpha above 0.0004 (about 0.04%). This value of 0.04% represents the average percentage outperformance of the strategy on a day-to-day basis, without penalizing negative returns. While 0.04% was the maximum value uncovered, this still does not represent a significant departure from zero. Overall, the mean value was almost exactly 0. See Chapter 2 for a thorough treatment of Jensen's Alpha.

The point of exploring trading strategy simulation, optimization, and then bootstrap simulation in this way had two purposes. First, I aimed to familiarize readers with the concepts in a reasonably simple fashion. Second, I aimed to show that strategies operating purely on daily price movements cannot produce statistically market-beating results.

There is a lot of potential exploration and improvement that remains to be done on the sample strategy we have been working with. It could even potentially be part of a winning trading strategy. I expect that readers who focus on extending and customizing this work will not have their ideas validated by the rigorous testing methods discussed in this chapter, so long as they only use end-of-day price data.

The remainder of this book will focus on integrating alternative data into trading strategies to discover market-beating returns. We will explore a variety of quantitative methods aimed at converting this alternative data into tradeable signals, and we will use the same methods discussed in this chapter to test their validity.

Chapter 6

Alternative Data

Alternative data is generally considered to be any non-traditional indicator of financial performance. By non-traditional, we mean that it is not among the traditional investor data toolkit that includes price history, fundamental data, and analyst recommendations. By indicator, we mean that the data itself does not need to be about dollar figures. The data itself is often a proxy for something that translates to financial performance. The financial performance metric that is most often proxied by alternative data is revenue.

6.1 Financial Reporting Schedules

The power of alternative data has a lot to do with when and how companies report financial performance. To explain why, we will start with an example.

Say, for sake of example, a powerful investor wants to estimate the revenue of Starbucks Coffee. He sees that Starbucks has about 30,000 coffee shops worldwide. This investor realizes that a good proxy of Starbuck's overall revenue is the number of customers that visit its stores. Different customers might spend different amounts of money, but, on average, each customer generates a certain amount of revenue for the business.

In order to estimate how many customers Starbucks gets on a daily basis, he sends 300 people to 300 randomly selected Starbucks locations around the globe to sit and watch the front doors. The "watchers" have one job. They are to count how many people enter the front door, every day, all day. Every night when they come home from watching the Starbucks all day, they email the number of customers they saw to an analyst at the headquarters.

The analyst at the headquarters has one job. He manages a massive spreadsheet that totals up the number of customers that enter the 300 Starbucks locations every day. That spreadsheet is alternative data, and it is probably really valuable alternative data. The data might look like the following in a `pandas` data frame.

```
            number_of_customers
2016-03-01               288343
2016-03-02               153540
2016-03-03               285703
2016-03-04                85651
2016-03-05                94570
...                         ...
2016-06-04               298062
2016-06-05               219089
2016-06-06               187542
2016-06-07               107151
2016-06-08               239065
```

This alternative data is probably *very* highly correlated with the actual daily revenue stream of Starbucks, so it should give the investor a competitive advantage. To understand why this information creates an advantage, we need to understand how public companies report financial performance.

Readers are likely familiar with 10K and 10Q reports published by public companies. In short, at least every quarter, a company issues an update on its financial performance either in the form of a 10K or a 10Q. The only difference between the reports is that one is a yearly update and the other is a quarterly update. They both constitute quarterly updates.

If a company's fiscal calendar starts on January 1st, they will likely release a 10K report for Q1 around May 15th, a full six week after the end of its first fiscal quarter, March 31st. There are exceptions and extensions granted occasionally, but this will be the case most of the time. This means that, in general, investors are not aware of the officially reported revenue until a full six weeks after that last bit of revenue was earned. For a company like Starbucks, where very small bits of revenue are earned every day, a coffee purchased on January 1st will not be reflected in public financial statements until a full 18 weeks later.

The length and sluggishness of the financial reporting process is one of the most important reasons that alternative data can confer a competitive advantage. If, for example, on January 1st, the world woke up and decided Starbucks coffee was absolutely disgusting, investors with access to alternative data would know first, whereas Wall Street would not find out for 18 weeks. Advance knowledge of such a massive change in consumer preferences would create a very good investment opportunity for those privy to this information.

Now, this is just a contrived example. We all know that if people suddenly started to revile Starbucks coffee, they would be complaining on social media, on the news, and at the kitchen table. There would be more than one way to figure out that people no longer liked Starbucks. Also, Starbucks itself is allowed to speak on its own behalf and provide its own revenue estimates directly to the public ahead of its filing deadlines. In reality, the source of the informational advantage is rarely so cut and dry, but my point stands. Alternative data can provide useful signals about financial performance.

6.2 Sources of Alternative Data

In the previous section, we discussed a contrived example where a powerful investor allocated tens of thousands of man-hours to building an alternative data set by hand. In real life, we typically just replace the people with technology. A single stationary camera running a computer vision algorithm could count the people instead. The resulting data set would be essentially the same.

The key to building effective alternative data sets is to figure out what inputs drive revenue for a business, then figure out how to measure those inputs. This line of thinking gives rise to a lot of the most commonly cited applications of alternative data. The most common examples include the following.

- Using satellite imagery to measure crop yields to trade crop futures and food companies.
- Using cameras to count foot traffic at any brick-and-mortar retail company.
- Tracking social media engagement for any product that has an active online community.

More obscure examples include the following.

- Interviewing employees regarding sales and financial health.
- Tracking flight patterns of activist investors to presuppose M&A activity.
- Obtaining retail sales data from retailers of products sold by the company.

All of these examples have documented use in the real world. Most of them provide proxies for raw revenue figures, but not all of them provide it at daily granularity as in our Starbucks example.

It should come as no surprise that these data sources are rare and expensive. Collecting alternative data on a specific company typically requires a custom technology infrastructure that can be expensive to develop and maintain. Thus, this book has provided some simulated alternative data.

6.3 Working with Alternative Data

In this book, we will work with a simulated set of alternative data. See the files in `/data/alternative_data/` of the project repository. These files correspond to the stock symbols in `/data/eod/` that we have been using thusfar. Just like how our end-of-day price data is very realistically simulated based on real stocks, our alternative data is simulated based on real revenue reports from those same stocks.

The alternative data we provide is also *very* clean – even unrealistically clean. The dates correspond exactly with those of the end-of-day stock data, so it can be concatenated with those data frames very easily. We have mysteriously named the column of alternative data `value`, because it is not important what underlying phenomena that value represents. All that is important is that the `value` represents a noisy real-time proxy of the current quarter's revenue, just like real alternative data.

We designed the book in this way because our primary goal is not to explore the significant data engineering task of developing an alternative data pipeline. Our primary our is to explore the signal processing and machine learning methodologies involved in translating alternative data into actionable trading signals. At the end, we will discuss how the simulation and optimization techniques developed thusfar can integrate machine learning strategies.

6.3.1 Exploring Our Simulated Data

See Listing 6.1 for methods of loading in our alternative data. It follows the same interface as our end-of-day data functions. Notice that our alternative data only spans 5 years, from 2015 through the end of 2019. Because both data frames use only trading days as rows, we can get the indexes to match up by chopping off everything before the start of the alternative data. We will do this frequently while working with this data.

```
from pypm import data_io
import numpy as np
import pandas as pd
from typing import List

# Load in everything
symbols: List[str] = data_io.get_all_symbols()
eod_data: pd.DataFrame = data_io.load_eod_matrix(symbols)
alt_data: pd.DataFrame = data_io.load_alternative_data_matrix(symbols)

# Our eod_data goes back 10 years, but our alt_data goes back 5 years
eod_data = eod_data[eod_data.index >= alt_data.index.min()]
assert np.all(eod_data.index == alt_data.index)
assert np.all(eod_data.columns == alt_data.columns)
```

Listing 6.1: Loading in alternative data

See Figures 6.1, 6.2, and 6.3 for a comparison of the alternative data time series to the closing price time series of AWU, BMG, and CUU.

See Listing 6.2 for some exploratory analysis of relationships between the alternative data and price series. See Figure 6.4 for the distribution of correlation coefficients of daily changes in price and alternative data values.

There does not seem to be a significant correlation between changes in the alternative data values and changes in the price series on a day-to-day basis. This is a worthwhile preliminary test to show how financial time series exhibit a low signal-to-noise ratio. Extracting meaningful signals from our revenue data will require more heavy-handed signal processing techniques.

```
from pypm import data_io, metrics
import numpy as np
```

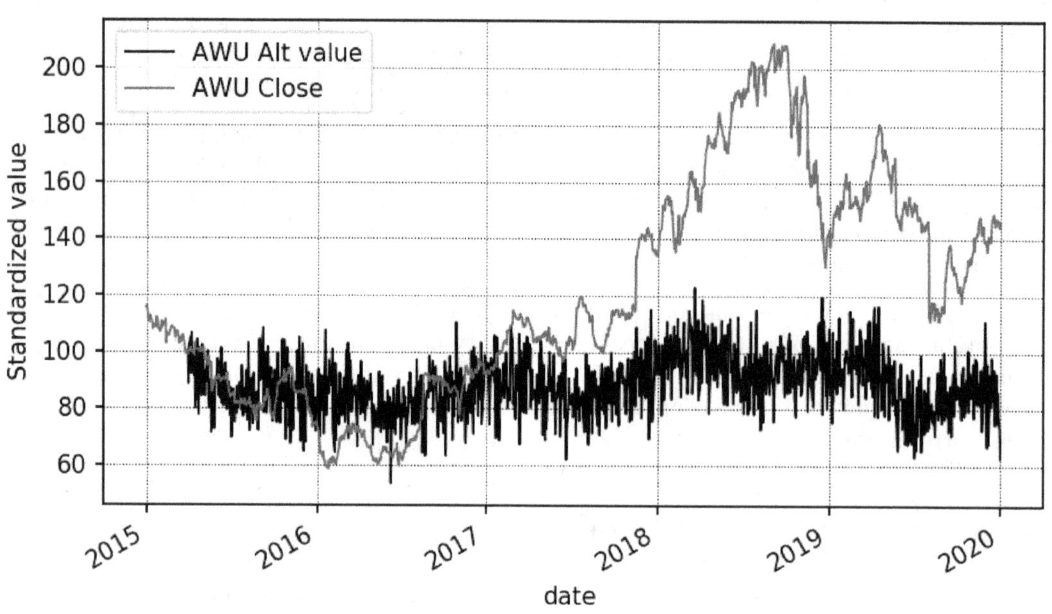

Figure 6.1: Alternative data vs. Close for AWU

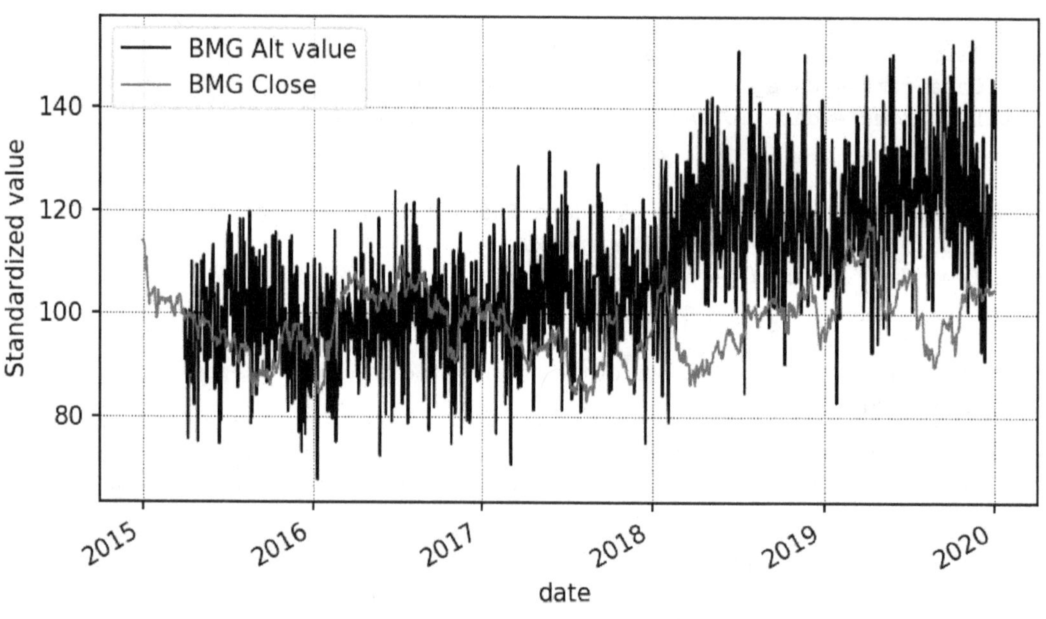

Figure 6.2: Alternative data vs. Close for BMG

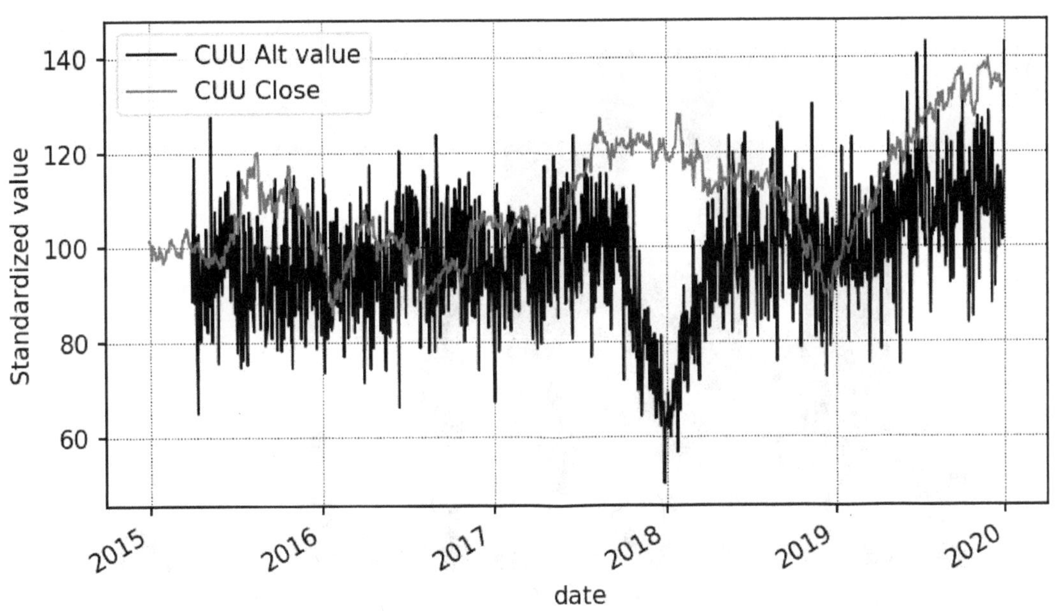

Figure 6.3: Alternative data vs. Close for CUU

```
import pandas as pd
from typing import List

# Load in everything
symbols: List[str] = data_io.get_all_symbols()
eod_data: pd.DataFrame = data_io.load_eod_matrix(symbols)
alt_data: pd.DataFrame = data_io.load_alternative_data_matrix(symbols)
eod_data = eod_data[eod_data.index >= alt_data.index.min()]

_calc_returns = metrics.calculate_log_return_series
_corr_by_symbol = dict()

for symbol in symbols:

    alt_series = alt_data[symbol].dropna()
    price_series = eod_data[symbol]

    if alt_series.empty:
        continue

    # Calculate returns, ensuring each series has the same index
    price_return_series = _calc_returns(price_series.loc[alt_series.index])
    alt_return_series = _calc_returns(alt_series)

    # Remove the NA at the front
    price_return_series = price_return_series.iloc[1:]
    alt_return_series = alt_return_series.iloc[1:]
```

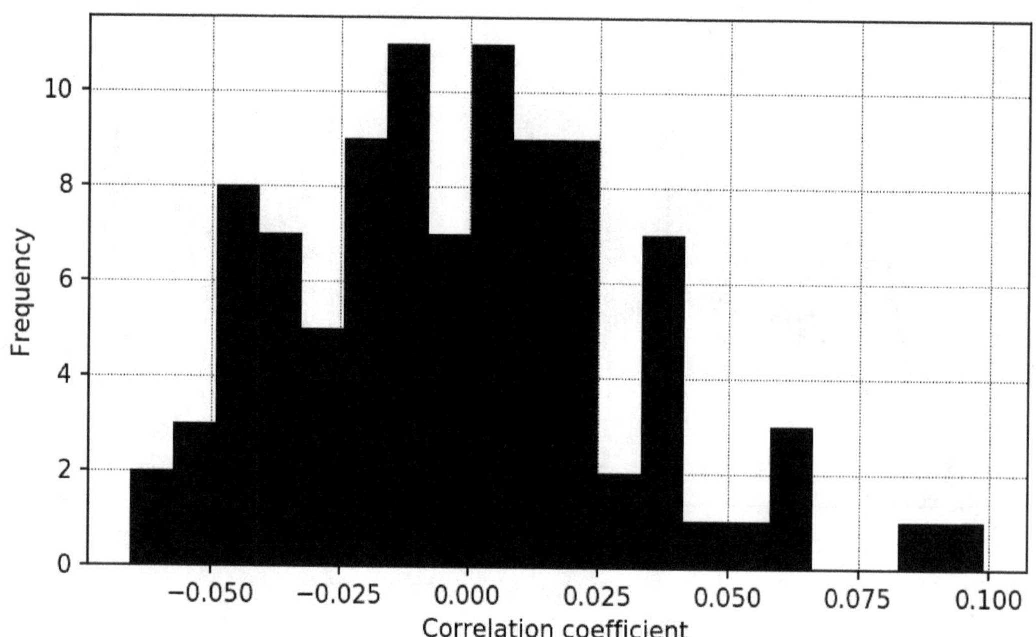

Figure 6.4: Correlation between changes in Alternative Data and Prices by Symbols

```
    # Calculate the correllation
    _corr = np.corrcoef(price_return_series, alt_return_series)

    # This element of the correlation matrix is the number we want
    _corr_by_symbol[symbol] = _corr[1,0]

# Describe results
results = pd.Series(_corr_by_symbol)
print(pd.DataFrame(results.describe()).T)
# Returns ...
#  count       mean       std       min       25%       50%     75%       max
#   97.0 -0.002539  0.032456 -0.065556 -0.024983 -0.003735  0.0174  0.099085
```

Listing 6.2: Exploratory analysis

6.4 Conclusion

The next chapter will cover signal processing methods required for building a machine learning model using the alternative data and price data. While there is much more exploratory analysis we could potentially do with this data, we will jump straight to those methods that make the most sense in the context of machine learning models.

Chapter 7

Machine Learning

In the last chapter, we introduced a simulated alternative data stream and discussed how it could be used to gain an informational advantage. After some cursory analysis, we discovered that there is no immediately observable or obvious relationship between the alternative data series and the end-of-day price series. In this chapter, we will explore machine learning methods to attempt to uncover meaningful relationships within the data.

This chapter will borrow heavily from the methods discussed in first five chapters of Advances in Financial Machine Learning (2018) by Dr. Marcos López de Prado, with the goal of contextualizing those methods into a reproducible machine learning pipeline. The beginning of López de Prado's book gives an excellent treatment of the ways in which financial machine learning differs from other machine learning applications. According to his book, while you can use existing frameworks like `scikit-learn`, the inputs and modeling parameters need to be modified significantly in order to generate meaningful signals on financial data.

Readers should be familiar with machine learning and somewhat familiar with `scikit-learn` in order to understand the material in this chapter. We will assume a working knowledge of machine learning terminology and discuss advanced configurations of `scikit-learn` models.

The topic of financial machine learning is deserving of its own book, much like the one written by López de Prado. Instead of attempting to cover the discipline of financial machine learning in depth, this chapter will discuss and implement some core principles with the goal of building a rudimentary financial machine learning pipeline. We will also attempt to point out any pitfalls or under-serviced topics that warrant additional research. Ultimately, the standard of reproducibility we have held up so far in this book will prevent us from properly exploring some topics in financial machine learning.

7.1 Generating Events

In the language of `sklearn`, a machine learning model needs a predictor array `X` where the columns represent predictors and the rows represent observations, and a target vector `y` with rows that correspond to `X`. Our data sets currently have columns that represent stock symbols and rows that represent end-of-day values of either prices or alternative data. One of the most difficult problems in financial machine learning is determining what a row of `X` represents.

We will argue that the rows of `X` should represent financial *events*. In the language of financial machine learning, an event represents a point in time where some data series exhibited interesting behavior. Regardless of what happens after the event, we choose to model the behavior of the price series following that point in time. In other words, each row of `X` will represent the predictors measured at points in time represented by events. In our application, `X` will be a `pd.DataFrame` with a date index of event dates.

In our example model, we will generate events by observing year-over-year deviations in the alternative data values. We will refer to these values casually as the *revenue series* throughout, because they proxy revenue earned by the company. We will use this series to generate events based on the assumption that positive or negative revenue surprises are a driver for price change, and our data gives us advance access to revenue data. In the context of the Starbucks example from the last chapter, observing year-over-year deviations in customer traffic would give us advance notice of revenue surprises. When developing a time series filter to identify these events, we want to balance between filtering noise and identifying signals.

We will use a method from López de Prado's book called the symmetric CUSUM filter to generate events on the revenue series. This filter keeps track of both positive and negative deviations from an expected value until they reach a user-defined threshold. When the threshold is met, the accumulator is reset to zero and the date is recorded as an event. I believe this is best explained through code and visualization, rather than through mathematical formulas.

See Listing 7.1 for our implementation. See Figure 7.1, 7.2, and 7.3 for visualizations of the internal mechanics.

```
# In pypm.filters
import numpy as np
import pandas as pd

def calculate_non_uniform_lagged_change(series: pd.Series, n_days: int):
    """
    Use pd.Series.searchsorted to measure the lagged change in a non-uniformly
    spaced time series over n_days of calendar time.
    """

    # Get mapping from now to n_days ago at every point
    _timedelta: pd.Timedelta = pd.Timedelta(days=n_days)
    _idx: pd.Series = series.index.searchsorted(series.index - _timedelta)
    _idx = _idx[_idx > 0]

    # Get the last len(series) - n_days values
    _series = series.iloc[-_idx.shape[0]:]

    # Build a padding of NA values
    _pad_length = series.shape[0] - _idx.shape[0]
    _na_pad = pd.Series(None, index=series.index[:_pad_length])

    # Get the corresonding lagged values
    _lagged_series = series.iloc[_idx]

    # Measure the difference
    _diff = pd.Series(_series.values-_lagged_series.values, index=_series.index)

    return pd.concat([_na_pad, _diff])


def calculate_cusum_events(series: pd.Series,
    filter_threshold: float) -> pd.DatetimeIndex:
    """
    Calculate symmetric cusum filter and corresponding events
    """

    event_dates = list()
```

```
    s_up = 0
    s_down = 0

    for date, price in series.items():
        s_up = max(0, s_up + price)
        s_down = min(0, s_down + price)

        if s_up > filter_threshold:
            s_up = 0
            event_dates.append(date)

        elif s_down < -filter_threshold:
            s_down = 0
            event_dates.append(date)

    return pd.DatetimeIndex(event_dates)

# In pypm.ml_model.events
from pypm import filters

def calculate_events_for_revenue_series(series: pd.Series,
    filter_threshold: float, lookback: int=365) -> pd.DatetimeIndex:
    """
    Calculate the symmetric cusum filter to generate events on YoY changes in
    the log revenue series
    """
    series = np.log(series)
    series = filters.calculate_non_uniform_lagged_change(series, lookback)
    return filters.calculate_cusum_events(series, filter_threshold)


def calculate_events(revenue_series: pd.Series):
    return calculate_events_for_revenue_series(
        revenue_series,
        filter_threshold=5,
        lookback=365,
    )
```

Listing 7.1: Symmetric CUSUM Filter on revenue series

Note that the CUSUM calculation is made on the year-over-year change in the revenue series. We can see from Figures 7.1 and 7.2 that the accumulators rise and fall when the YoY change is above or below zero on average for a significant period of time. We can also see that, when the YoY revenue series spends a lot of time above or below zero, the CUSUM filter may generate numerous events very close to one another. To some extent, this is an intended behavior. Although, if events are generated so frequently that they are indistinguishable from a daily or weekly series, you may want to increase the value of `filter_threshold`. We will further adjust for cases when events are generated too close to one another in the labeling step.

Note the dates and frequency of the events plotted against the price series in Figure 7.3. You may be tempted to see a pattern within these signals, but you should refrain. Remember that the events are not generated for predictive purposes. They are simply a list of times at which an interesting signal occurred. We are leaving it up to the machine learning algorithm down the line to predict the significance and the direction of the price move that occurred after the event.

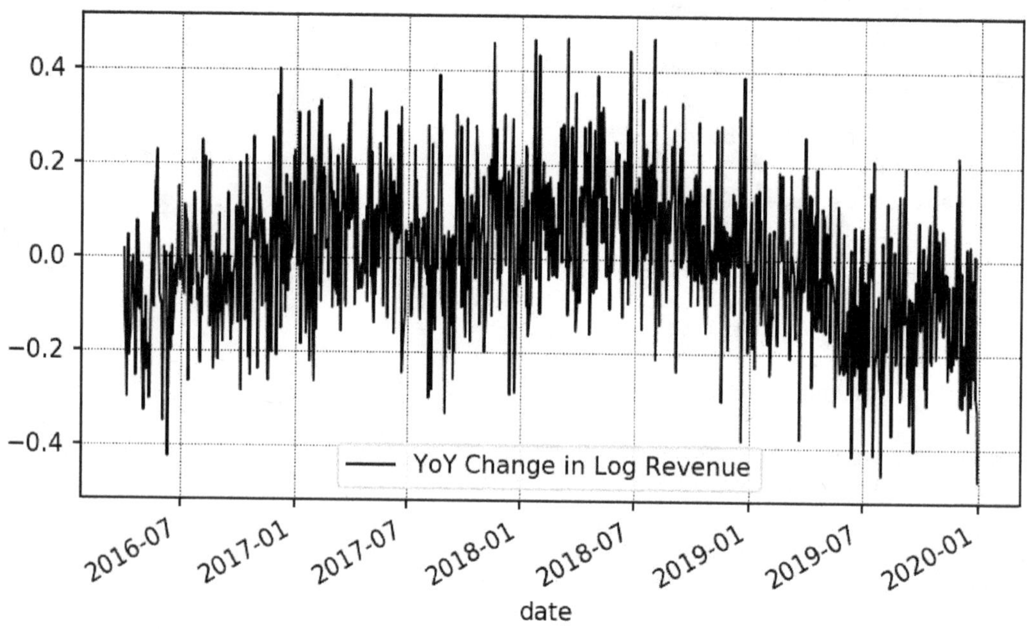

Figure 7.1: Year-over-year change in revenue on AWU

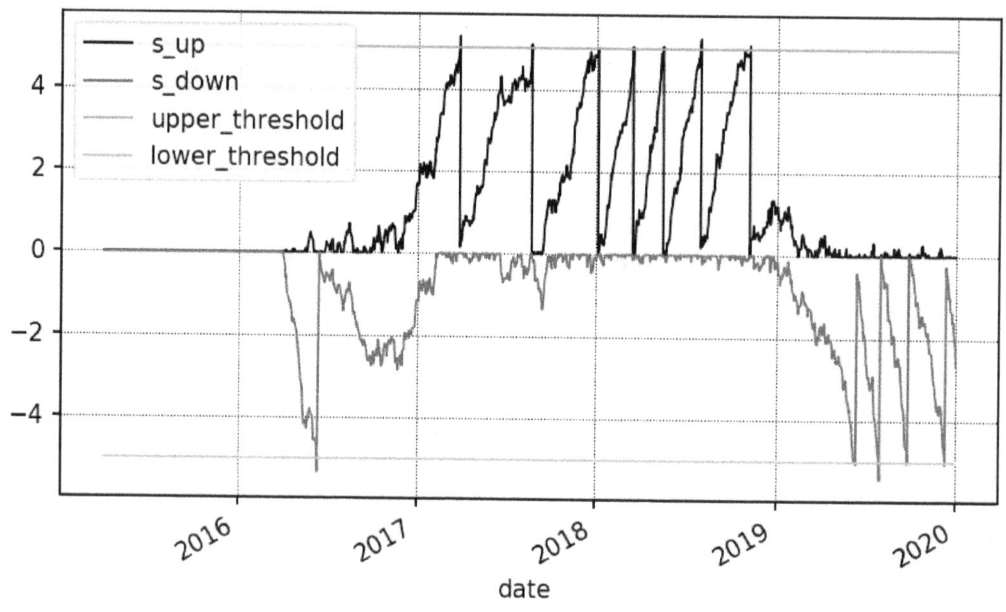

Figure 7.2: CUSUM accumulators on AWU revenue

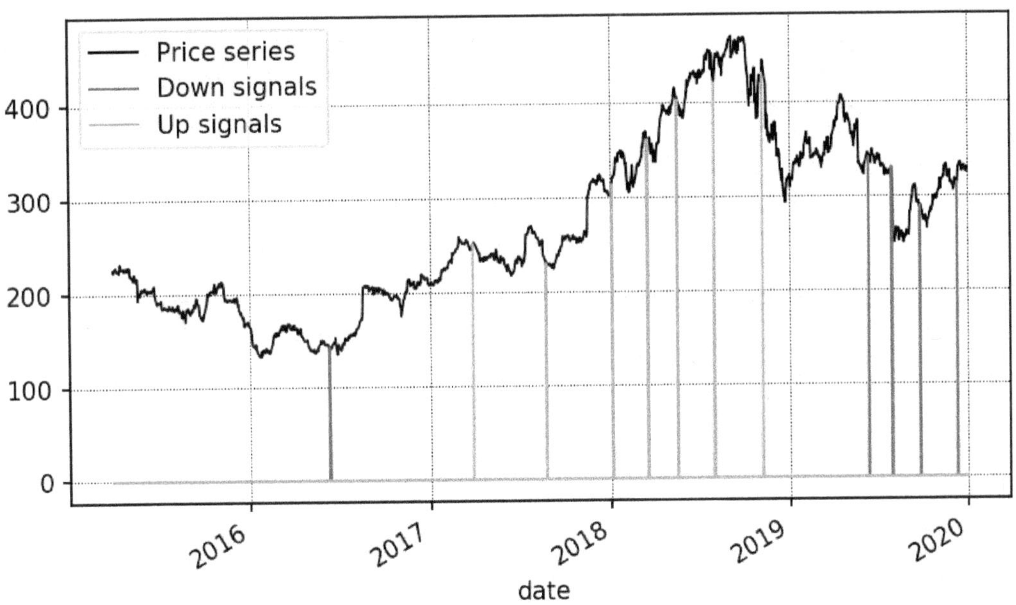

Figure 7.3: CUSUM events on AWU revenue

7.2 Generating Labels

In the language of **sklearn**, the labels represent the target vector y. Now that we have generated events, we can observe the behavior in the price series that occurs after each event and assign it a label. Following the methods of López de Prado, we will generate labels for a classification problem with three possible outcomes, $\{-1, 0, 1\}$, representing a move down, a move sideways, and a move up in the price series, respectively. We will adopt a modification of the Triple Barrier Method to assign the labels.

The triple barrier method defines three barriers relative to the price on the event date. For some percentage change k and some length of time T, we have the following.

- An upper barrier representing a $+k\%$ move in the price, corresponding to 1.
- A lower barrier representing a $-k\%$ move in the price, corresponding to -1.
- A vertical barrier representing a maximum amount of time, T, allowed for the price series to hit another barrier first, corresponding to 0.

In other words, the first barrier that is hit determines the value of the label. In practice, we will set k dynamically based on the volatility of the underlying price series. As part of calculating the triple barrier labels, we will also keep track of when the labels started (same as the event dates) and the end dates. We will use these dates later to modify the weights of our machine learning model.

```
# See pypm.labels
import numpy as np
import pandas as pd
from typing import Tuple

def compute_triple_barrier_labels(
    price_series: pd.Series,
    event_index: pd.Series,
```

```
    time_delta_days: int,
    upper_delta: float=None,
    lower_delta: float=None,
    vol_span: int=20,
    upper_z: float=None,
    lower_z: float=None,
    upper_label: int=1,
    lower_label: int=-1) -> Tuple[pd.Series, pd.Series]:
    """
    Calculate event labels according to the triple-barrier method.

    Return a series with both the original events and the labels. Labels 1, 0,
    and -1 correspond to upper barrier breach, vertical barrier breach, and
    lower barrier breach, respectively.

    Also return series where the index is the start date of the label and the
    values are the end dates of the label.
    """

    timedelta = pd.Timedelta(days=time_delta_days)
    series = pd.Series(np.log(price_series.values), index=price_series.index)

    # A list with elements of {-1, 0, 1} indicating the outcome of the events
    labels = list()
    label_dates = list()

    if upper_z or lower_z:
        volatility = series.ewm(span=vol_span).std()
        volatility *= np.sqrt(time_delta_days / vol_span)

    for event_date in event_index:
        date_barrier = event_date + timedelta

        start_price = series.loc[event_date]
        log_returns = series.loc[event_date:date_barrier] - start_price

        # First element of tuple is 1 or -1 indicating upper or lower barrier
        # Second element of tuple is first date when barrier was crossed
        candidates: List[Tuple[int, pd.Timestamp]] = list()

        # Add the first upper or lower delta crosses to candidates
        if upper_delta:
            _date = log_returns[log_returns > upper_delta].first_valid_index()
            if _date:
                candidates.append((upper_label, _date))

        if lower_delta:
            _date = log_returns[log_returns < lower_delta].first_valid_index()
            if _date:
                candidates.append((lower_label, _date))

        # Add the first upper_z and lower_z crosses to candidates
        if upper_z:
            upper_barrier = upper_z * volatility[event_date]
```

```
            _date = log_returns[log_returns > upper_barrier].first_valid_index()
            if _date:
                candidates.append((upper_label, _date))

        if lower_z:
            lower_barrier = lower_z * volatility[event_date]
            _date = log_returns[log_returns < lower_barrier].first_valid_index()
            if _date:
                candidates.append((lower_label, _date))

        if candidates:
            # If any candidates, return label for first date
            label, label_date = min(candidates, key=lambda x: x[1])
        else:
            # If there were no candidates, time barrier was touched
            label, label_date = 0, date_barrier

        labels.append(label)
        label_dates.append(label_date)

    label_series = pd.Series(labels, index=event_index)
    event_spans = pd.Series(label_dates, index=event_index)

    return label_series, event_spans


# See pypm.ml_model.labels
from typing import Tuple
from pypm import labels

def calculate_labels(price_series, event_index) -> Tuple[pd.Series, pd.Series]:
    """
    Calculate labels based on the triple barrier method. Return a series of
    event labels index by event start date, and return a series of event end
    dates indexed by event start date.
    """

    # Remove event that don't have a proper chance to materialize
    time_delta_days = 90
    max_date = price_series.index.max()
    cutoff = max_date - pd.Timedelta(days=time_delta_days)
    event_index = event_index[event_index <= cutoff]

    # Use triple barrier method
    event_labels, event_spans = labels.compute_triple_barrier_labels(
        price_series,
        event_index,
        time_delta_days=time_delta_days,
        upper_z=1.8,
        lower_z=-1.8,
    )

    return event_labels, event_spans
```

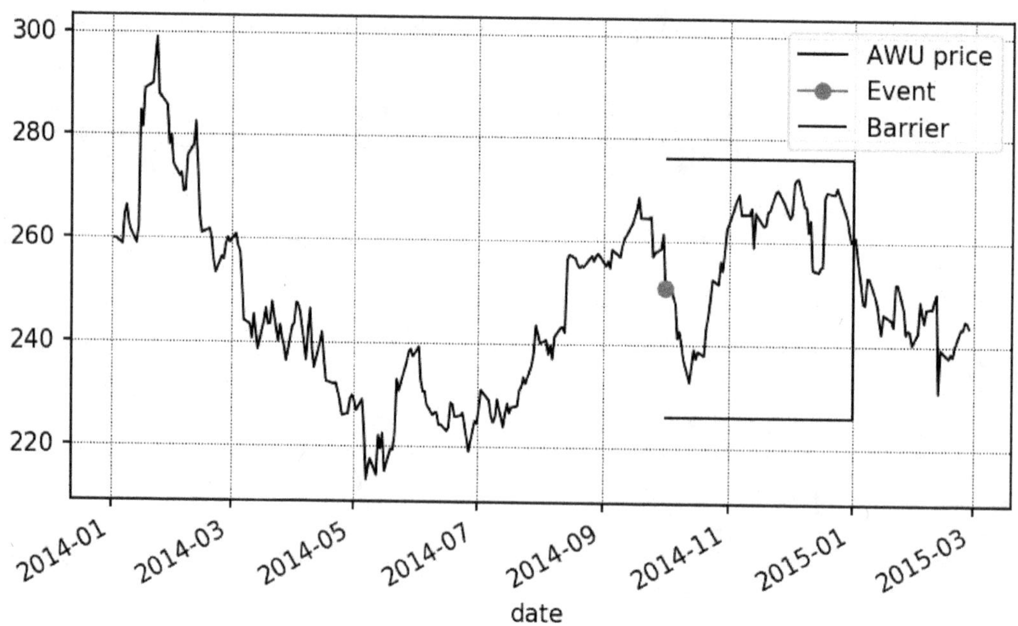

Figure 7.4: Triple Barrier Example on AWU

Listing 7.2: Computing Triple Barrier Labels

See Listing 7.2 for computation of the triple barrier method. In this implementation, `lower_delta` and `upper_delta` represent $-k\%$ and $+k\%$, respectively. These parameters let you specify a fixed percentage change for the barriers. The variables `upper_z` and `lower_z` represent the upper and lower barriers as multiples of standardized volatility. Although these parameters represent different types of upper and lower barriers, they can all be set simultaneously due to the way the algorithm is programmed. The variable `time_delta_days` represents the distance from the event to the vertical barrier in days.

The function at the bottom of Listing 7.2 shows a reasonable application, where events evolve over a maximum of 90 days, and the barriers are set as 1.8 standard deviations above and below the event price.

See Figure 7.4 for a visualization of a triple barrier for an arbitrary event on AWU with +/- 10% horizontal barriers and a 90 day vertical barrier. In Figure 7.4, the vertical barrier was triggered, resulting in a label value of 0.

At this point, we have generated events and weights. In terms of building `X` and `y`, we have finished building `y`, the labels. In the process, we have built a date index for `y`, the events, that will also serve as the date index for `X`.

7.3 Generating Weights

Most model-fitting frameworks and algorithms provide some opportunity to set weights. The weights vector `w` has the same shape and index as `y` and determines how important each label is to the fitting and scoring of the model. In most machine learning applications, observations are assumed to have to been drawn from an independent identically distributed random variable (IID), thus justifying a default weighting vector of all ones.

Weights can be adjusted at the researcher's discretion to amplify or dampen certain observations that might be desirable for the model's performance. There is no precise formula on how to set weights in machine learning. Changes to the weights are typically based on a researcher's intuition about the problem. Clever usage of creative weighting schemes can substantially improve a model, especially in the presence of obviously non-IID data. We will discuss one such method in this section to attempt to correct for the non-IID nature of our event generation and labeling methods.

In the first section of this chapter, we discussed an event generation method that looks only at the revenue stream of the underlying asset to calculate dates where something interesting ought to have occurred afterwards. Technically, this event generation process has no boundaries on how frequently it can generate events. The parameters we supplied to it are only considered well-conditioned because they produce a reasonable pattern of events *most* of the time, as in Figure 7.3.

In a previous section of this chapter, we discussed a labeling method that generates a label based on the materialization of price movements following an event. The time span that can pass between the event and the price that generates the label can be between 1 and 90 calendar days in our parameterization.

We will call the time that passes between an event and the generation of a label an *event span*. See the output of Listing 7.2. The second return argument to the function is a `pd.Series` called `event_spans` containing the event date and the label generation date.

In our current setup, the event spans allow for overlaps. In other words, nothing is preventing a new event from being generated on a stock symbol during the event span of another. In some cases where the revenue series varies significantly, you will see numerous event spans materializing at the same point in time. Since each event represents a row in our machine learning model, it would be possible for 10 events materializing over a single stock in a single 90 day period to account for 10 rows in our model. As researchers, we know that this would create a gross misrepresentation of the importance of those 90 days on that stock within our model. We can use creative weighting schemes to correct this.

López de Prado suggests weighting observations according to their average uniqueness within the data set. In order to arrive at average uniqueness, we need to first define concurrency. The concurrency of an event span at time t is simply the total number of event spans that include time t for a stock symbol. In our previous example where 10 event spans are materializing at the same time, each of those event spans has a concurrency value of 10 at that time. The average uniqueness is then defined as the reciprocal of the harmonic average of the event span's concurrency values. The average uniqueness values will then serve as our weights.

The weights can be modified further to encourage the models to focus on specific types of labels. This is discussed further in López de Prado's book. We will refrain from modifying the weights any further after calculating the average uniqueness values.

```python
# See pypm.weights
import numpy as np
import pandas as pd
from scipy.stats import hmean

def calculate_uniqueness(event_spans: pd.Series,
    price_index: pd.Series) -> pd.Series:
    """
    event_spans is a series with an index of start dates and values of end dates
    of a label.

    price_index is an index of underlying dates for the event

    Returns a series of uniqueness values that can be used as weights, indexed
    as the event start dates. Weights may need to be standardized again before
    training.
    """
```

```
    # Create a binary data frame
    # value is 1 during event span and 0 otherwise
    columns = range(event_spans.shape[0])
    df = pd.DataFrame(0, index=price_index, columns=columns)

    for i, (event_start, event_end) in enumerate(event_spans.items()):
        df[i].loc[event_start:event_end] += 1

    # Compute concurrency over event span then calculate uniqueness
    uniquenesses = list()
    for i, (event_start, event_end) in enumerate(event_spans.items()):
        concurrency: pd.Series = df.loc[event_start:event_end].sum(axis=1)
        uniqueness = 1 / hmean(concurrency)
        uniquenesses.append(uniqueness)

    return pd.Series(uniquenesses, index=event_spans.index)

# See pypm.ml_model.weights
import numpy as np
import pandas as pd

from pypm.weights import calculate_uniqueness

def calculate_weights(event_spans: pd.Series,
    price_index: pd.Series) -> pd.Series:
    return calculate_uniqueness(event_spans, price_index)
```

Listing 7.3: Computing average uniqueness

See Figure 7.5 for the histogram of weight values calculated on our event spans. We can see that about 400 of them are not concurrent with anything else, with a weight value of 1, while hundreds are highly concurrent.

At this point, we have completely specified the labels `y` and the weights `w`. We have also specified the date index of `X`. To build out `X`, we will start creating features.

7.4 Computing Features

Computing features to build out `X` is relatively simple in the idyllic scenario we have established for ourselves. We only have two data streams, the alternative data and the price data, on which to build features. See Listing 7.4 for our code to build features on our data streams.

The decision to settle on these features came from various experiments with feature importance on our machine learning model, which we will discuss in the following section. Our features mainly consist of lagged changes on a smoothed series of prices, revenue, and volatility.

```
import numpy as np
import pandas as pd

from pypm import indicators, filters, metrics

_calc_delta = filters.calculate_non_uniform_lagged_change
_calc_ma = indicators.calculate_simple_moving_average
_calc_log_return = metrics.calculate_log_return_series
```

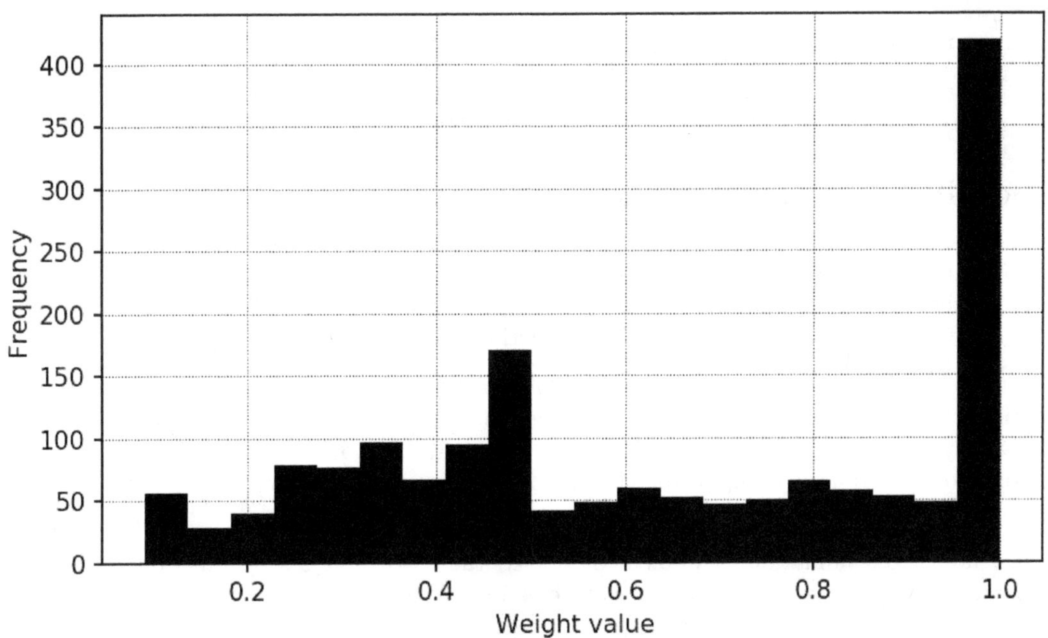

Figure 7.5: Histogram of weights on our event spans

```
def _calc_rolling_vol(series, n):
    return series.rolling(n).std() * np.sqrt(252 / n)

def calculate_features(price_series, revenue_series) -> pd.DataFrame:
    """
    Calculate any and all potentially useful features. Return as a dataframe.
    """

    log_revenue = np.log(revenue_series)
    log_prices = np.log(price_series)

    log_revenue_ma = _calc_ma(log_revenue, 10)
    log_prices_ma = _calc_ma(log_prices, 10)

    log_returns = _calc_log_return(price_series)

    features_by_name = dict()

    for i in [7, 30, 90, 180, 360]:

        rev_feature = _calc_delta(log_revenue_ma, i)
        price_feature = _calc_delta(log_prices_ma, i)
        vol_feature = _calc_rolling_vol(log_returns, i)

        features_by_name.update({
            f'{i}_day_revenue_delta': rev_feature,
            f'{i}_day_return': price_feature,
            f'{i}_day_vol': vol_feature,
```

```
    })

    features_df = pd.DataFrame(features_by_name)
    return features_df
```

Listing 7.4: Computing features

7.5 Modeling and Cross-Validation

When experimenting with machine learning models to determine the appropriate mix of features, event parameters, and label parameters, we will look at the feature importances and the cross-validation accuracy. To develop a good workflow, you should have a single function that calculates all of this and prints diagnostic information. See Listing 7.5.

See the function `calculate_model`. We use a `RandomForestClassifier` here because it is known to be a robust decision tree classifier. We then use a multicore cross-validation routine defined above it to compute the fit diagnostics. It is not important that readers understand exactly how the `joblib` multicore implementation works in order to understand the code.

To understand how cross-validation is implemented, see the `_fit_and_score` function. Simple cross-validation is purely a matter of subsetting `X`, `y`, and `w` into both train and test sets based on a set of randomly generated indexes and returning a single out-of-sample score from the fit. We run a repeated K-fold cross-validation in order to get a larger sample of out-of-sample scores.

The out-of-sample (OOS) accuracy of the model tells us how well the model predicts data it has not been trained on, but it does not tell us why. To better understand that, we look to the feature importances. The feature importances are computed internally as part of the fitting procedure of the `RandomForestClassifier`. They tell us how far each feature goes in improving the predictive accuracy of a node in the tree.

```
# See pypm.ml_model.model
import numpy as np
import pandas as pd

from sklearn.ensemble import RandomForestClassifier
from sklearn.model_selection import RepeatedKFold
from sklearn.base import clone

from joblib import Parallel, delayed

# Number of jobs to run in parallel
# Set to number of computer cores to use
N_JOBS = 10
N_SPLITS = 5
N_REPEATS = 4

def _fit_and_score(classifier, X, y, w, train_index, test_index, i) -> float:
    """
    The function used by joblib to split, train, and score cross validations
    """
    X_train = X.iloc[train_index]
    X_test = X.iloc[test_index]

    y_train = y.iloc[train_index]
    y_test = y.iloc[test_index]
```

```
    w_train = w.iloc[train_index]
    w_test = w.iloc[test_index]

    classifier.fit(X_train, y_train, w_train)
    score = classifier.score(X_test, y_test, w_test)

    print(f'Finished {i} ({100*score:.1f}%)')

    return score

def repeated_k_fold(classifier, X, y, w) -> np.ndarray:
    """
    Perform repeated k-fold cross validation on a classifier. Spread fitting
    job over multiple computer cores.
    """
    n_jobs = N_JOBS

    n_splits = N_SPLITS
    n_repeats = N_REPEATS

    total_fits =  n_splits * n_repeats

    _k_fold = RepeatedKFold(n_splits=n_splits, n_repeats=n_repeats)

    print(f'Fitting {total_fits} models {n_jobs} at a time ...')
    print()

    parallel = Parallel(n_jobs=n_jobs)
    scores = parallel(
        delayed(_fit_and_score)(
            clone(classifier), X, y, w, train_index, test_index, i
        ) for i, (train_index, test_index) in enumerate(_k_fold.split(X))
    )

    return np.array(scores)


def calculate_model(df: pd.DataFrame) -> RandomForestClassifier:
    """
    Given a dataframe with a y column, weights column, and predictor columns
    with arbitrary names, cross-validated and fit a classifier. Print
    diagnostics.
    """
    classifier = RandomForestClassifier(n_estimators=100)

    # Separate data
    predictor_columns = [
        c for c in df.columns.values if not c in ('y', 'weights')
    ]
    X = df[predictor_columns]
    y = df['y']
    w = df['weights']

    # Fit cross validation
```

```
    scores = repeated_k_fold(classifier, X, y, w)

    # Get a full dataset fit for importance scores
    classifier.fit(X, y, w)

    # Compute diagnostics
    _imp = classifier.feature_importances_
    importance_series = pd.Series(_imp, index=predictor_columns)
    importance_series = importance_series.sort_values(ascending=False)

    # baseline accuracy is the best value achievable with a constant guess
    baseline = np.max(y.value_counts() / y.shape[0])

    # Compute a rough confidence interval for the improvement
    mean_score = scores.mean()
    std_score = scores.std()

    upper_bound = mean_score + 2 * std_score
    lower_bound = mean_score - 2 * std_score
    ibounds = (lower_bound - baseline, upper_bound - baseline)

    print('Feature importances')
    for col, imp in importance_series.items():
        print(f'{col:24} {imp:>.3f}')
    print()

    print('Cross validation scores')
    print(np.round(100 * scores, 1))
    print()

    print(f'Baseline accuracy {100*baseline:.1f}%')
    print(f'OOS accuracy {100*mean_score:.1f}% +/- {200 * scores.std():.1f}%')
    print(f'Improvement {100*(ibounds[0]):.1f} to {100*(ibounds[1]):.1f}%')
    print()

    return classifier
```

Listing 7.5: Modeling and cross-validation

Tying all of the components together, we get Listing 7.6.

```
# See fit_alternative_data_model.py
import os
import pandas as pd
import numpy as np
from typing import Dict

from joblib import dump

from pypm.ml_model.data_io import load_data
from pypm.ml_model.events import calculate_events
from pypm.ml_model.labels import calculate_labels
from pypm.ml_model.features import calculate_features
from pypm.ml_model.model import calculate_model
from pypm.ml_model.weights import calculate_weights
```

```
SRC_DIR = os.path.dirname(os.path.abspath(__file__))

if __name__ == '__main__':

    # All the data we have to work with
    symbols, eod_data, alt_data = load_data()

    # The ML dataframe for each symbol, to be combined later
    df_by_symbol: Dict[str, pd.DataFrame] = dict()

    # Build ML dataframe for each symbol
    for symbol in symbols:

        # Get revenue and price series
        revenue_series = alt_data[symbol].dropna()
        price_series = eod_data[symbol].dropna()
        price_index = price_series.index

        # Get events, labels, weights, and features
        event_index = calculate_events(revenue_series)
        event_labels, event_spans = calculate_labels(price_series, event_index)
        weights = calculate_weights(event_spans, price_index)
        features_df = calculate_features(price_series, revenue_series)

        # Subset features by event dates
        features_on_events = features_df.loc[event_index]

        # Convert labels and events to a data frame
        labels_df = pd.DataFrame(event_labels)
        labels_df.columns = ['y']

        # Converts weights to a data frame
        weights_df = pd.DataFrame(weights)
        weights_df.columns = ['weights']

        # Concatenate features to labels
        df = pd.concat([features_on_events, weights_df, labels_df], axis=1)
        df_by_symbol[symbol] = df

    # Create final ML dataframe
    df = pd.concat(df_by_symbol.values(), axis=0)
    df.sort_index(inplace=True)
    df.dropna(inplace=True)
    print(df)

    # Fit the model
    classifier = calculate_model(df)

    # Save the model
    dump(classifier, os.path.join(SRC_DIR, 'ml_model.joblib'))

# Returns ...
#            7_day_revenue_delta  7_day_return  7_day_vol  ...
```

```
# 2016-06-07              -0.000721    0.019520   0.096002  ...
# 2016-06-08               0.029827    0.025005   0.113246  ...
# 2016-06-08              -0.046427    0.013868   0.051878  ...
# 2016-06-09               0.001558    0.032410   0.064574  ...
# 2016-06-10               0.004933    0.011751   0.045105  ...
# ...                           ...         ...        ...  ...
# 2019-09-30              -0.031956   -0.008562   0.072845  ...
# 2019-10-01              -0.074244   -0.018469   0.053665  ...
# 2019-10-01               0.009513   -0.015659   0.094087  ...
# 2019-10-02               0.012819   -0.008300   0.062938  ...
# 2019-10-02               0.003023    0.015749   0.043320  ...
#
# [1563 rows x 17 columns]
# Fitting 20 models 10 at a time ...
#
# ...
# ...
# ...
#
# Feature importances
# 30_day_return           0.099
# 7_day_return            0.097
# 30_day_vol              0.073
# 90_day_return           0.068
# 360_day_vol             0.066
# 360_day_revenue_delta   0.064
# 360_day_return          0.063
# 180_day_return          0.063
# 180_day_revenue_delta   0.060
# 90_day_vol              0.060
# 180_day_vol             0.060
# 7_day_vol               0.059
# 7_day_revenue_delta     0.057
# 90_day_revenue_delta    0.057
# 30_day_revenue_delta    0.055
#
# Cross validation scores
# ...
#
# Baseline accuracy 42.2%
# OOS accuracy 52.4% +/- 5.3%
# Improvement 4.9 to 15.6%
#
```

Listing 7.6: Machine learning pipeline

From the terminal output of our `calculate_model` function we can see the model made an accuracy improvement over the baseline of about 10% in out-of-sample tests. We can also see that multiple features of the price series have high importance, including the near-term volatility and returns on the asset. Further, we can see that most important revenue feature by far is the YoY change in revenue. This is consistent with our expectations, considering that investors tend to focus on YoY changes in revenue. It is also consistent with our expectations that short-term changes in revenue are among the least important features.

There might be more worthwhile feature exploration to do on our data set, especially if readers choose to take advantage of open, high, low, and volume data in our end-of-day simulated data.

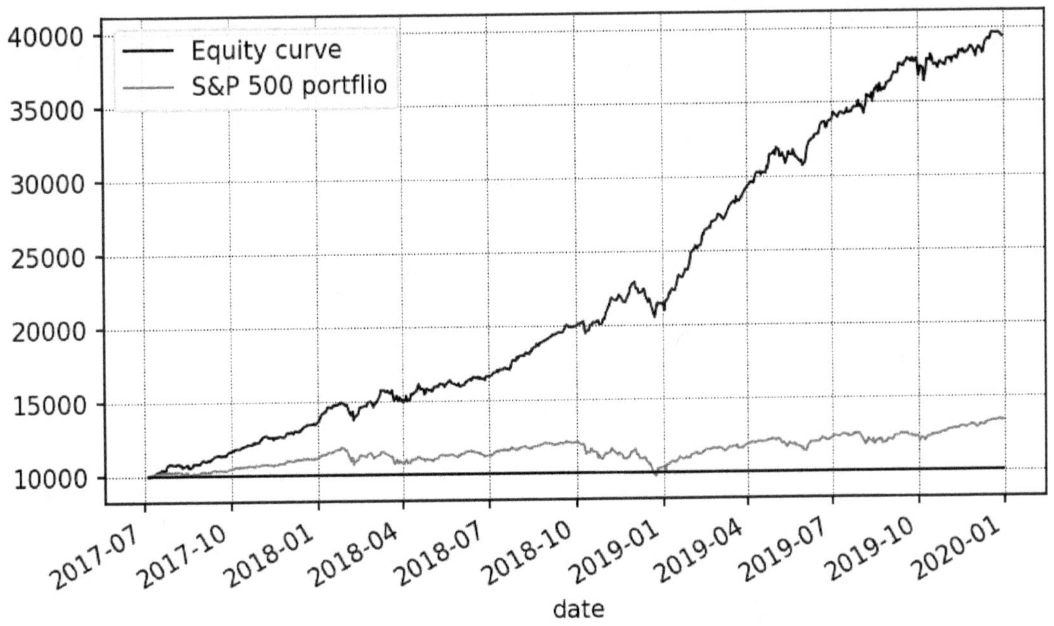

Figure 7.6: Equity curve vs. S&P 500 on overfit model

7.6 Simulating Trading Performance

For sake of completeness, we will show the code required to translate a machine learning model into a trading signal using our existing simulator we built in Chapter 4. In addition, this section will serve as an example of what an overfit machine learning model can accomplish when predicting in-sample data. It is very easy to overfit a machine learning model given the quantity and character of data we are working with. For example, fitting a `RandomForestClassifier` to our data set with `n_estimators=20` can achieve an in-sample prediction accuracy of 100%. Thus, we will expect to see unrealistically high performance on the trading simulation. See Listing 7.7 for the implementation. See Figure 7.6 for the equity curve compared to the S&P 500.

```
import pandas as pd
import numpy as np

import os
from joblib import load

from pypm.ml_model.data_io import load_data
from pypm.ml_model.signals import calculate_signals

from pypm import metrics, simulation

SRC_DIR = os.path.dirname(os.path.abspath(__file__))

def simulate_portfolio():

    # All the data we have to work with
    symbols, eod_data, alt_data = load_data()
```

```
    # Load classifier from file
    classifier = load(os.path.join(SRC_DIR, 'ml_model.joblib'))

    # Generate signals from classifier
    print('Calculating signals ...')
    signal = calculate_signals(classifier, symbols, eod_data, alt_data)

    # Get rid of eod_data before valid signals
    first_signal_date = signal.first_valid_index()
    eod_data = eod_data[eod_data.index > first_signal_date]

    # Set the preference to increase by row, so new trades are preferred
    print('Calculating preference matrix ...')
    preference = pd.DataFrame(
        np.random.random(eod_data.shape),
        columns=eod_data.columns,
        index=eod_data.index,
    )

    # Run the simulator
    simulator = simulation.SimpleSimulator(
        initial_cash=10000,
        max_active_positions=10,
        percent_slippage=0.0005,
        trade_fee=1,
    )
    simulator.simulate(eod_data, signal, preference)

    # Print results
    simulator.portfolio_history.print_position_summaries()
    simulator.print_initial_parameters()
    simulator.portfolio_history.print_summary()
    simulator.portfolio_history.plot()
    simulator.portfolio_history.plot_benchmark_comparison()

if __name__ == '__main__':
    simulate_portfolio()

# Returns ...
# Initial Cash: $10000
# Maximum Number of Assets: 10
#
# Equity: $45455.68
# Percent Return: 354.56%
# S&P 500 Return: 33.80%
#
# Number of trades: 291
# Average active trades: 9.89
#
# CAGR: 83.75%
# S&P 500 CAGR: 12.43%
# Excess CAGR: 71.32%
#
```

```
# Annualized Volatility: 14.44%
# Sharpe Ratio: 5.80
# Jensen's Alpha: 0.002018
#
# Dollar Max Drawdown: $1892.59
# Percent Max Drawdown: 8.60%
# Log Max Drawdown Ratio: 1.42
#
```

Listing 7.7: Simulation with machine learning model

Note that we use a random preference matrix in our simulation. The machine learning model generates signals with the framework we built in Chapter 4, in the sense that it outputs elements in $\{-1, 0, 1\}$, but we do not have an immediate solution for setting a preference value in the case of an overabundance of signals. We will not explore this topic, because we know that the model we are working with is an overfit with nearly perfect predictive accuracy. The reason for sharing Listing 7.7 is to give an idea of how to apply a machine learning model into a multi-asset strategy framework like the one we discussed.

Note how the simulation's CAGR is 83% over a 2.5 year period where the S&P 500's CAGR is 12% over that same period, even when the preference matrix is filled with random noise. The overfit model knows exactly which stocks will move and its predicts their movements nearly perfectly because we are using in-sample data.

7.7 Potential Pitfalls

This section will discuss potential pitfalls in our machine learning pipeline and various under-serviced topics that warrant further research.

7.7.1 Limited Data

Note that our price data set spans 10 years of daily data consisting of about 2,500 observations per symbol. In addition, our alternative data spans 5 years of daily revenue data consisting of about 1,250 observations per symbol. Machine learning models do not accept or work with `None` or `np.nan` values, so we have to drop every row that contains a null value after event generation, labeling, and featurization. What we are left with is about 2.5 years of valid of training data to work with, which can be reduced even further under certain cross-validation methods.

Most of the pitfalls in the machine learning pipeline presented here are issues that cannot be solved given the quantity and character of data we are working with. In some respects, the structure of the simulated data we present in this book is intractable for use in a production trading system. These are the limitations presented to us when writing against the standard of reproducibility sought in this book.

7.7.2 Better Cross-Validation

There is an opportunity to perform better cross-validation with a method that is particularly relevant to financial time series. Earlier in this chapter, we discussed how observing event spans to create better weighting schemes can improve our model. The reason we need to modify our weights arises from the overlapping nature of our events and our desire to avoid double- or triple-counting the significance of a label. The issue of overlapping labels gives rise to similar issues in cross-validation.

The purpose of cross-validation is to hold specific data back from the machine learning model in order to develop a better sense of the *generalization error*. This term refers broadly to the value to which both the out-of-sample error and the walk-forward prediction error should converge to under ideal circumstances.

The way we perform cross-validation in the code in this chapter undoubtedly introduces significant data leakage into the model and calls into question whether or not we arrived at the true generalization error. It also calls into question whether or not our model is a trivial act of overfitting. Proper cross-validation in a financial time series context would have to account for overlapping labels.

For example, consider a section of the price series that had 10 events generated within 90 days that last an average of 45 days. Some of those events occur within days of each other. All of the events have high concurrency and share some sections of the event span with one another. If our cross-validation scheme pulls random rows from our training data set without regard for this overlap, an in-sample label generated one day could be used to predict an out-of-sample label generated in the same week. The model would undoubtedly do a good job at predicting the out-of-sample label because it has seen approximately 90% of the event span before, in the sample.

To some extent, the weighting scheme we discussed in this chapter helps overcome the inflated score naive cross-validation would cause, but it could still lead to false discoveries. It would be preferable if we could entirely prevent data leakage in our cross-validation step. Such methods exist, and readers are encouraged to read López de Prado's discussion of *purging* and cross-validation in the aforementioned book. Unfortunately, our data is not conducive to these methods because of its brevity and lengthy lookback period.

7.7.3 Better Simulation

Our problem with cross-validation of model fitting also prevents us from performing proper cross-validated trading simulations. Readers are directed to see López de Prado's discussion of backtesting for more on this topic. Running a proper out-of-sample trading simulation requires a form of purging that is too taxing on our already brief data.

7.7.4 Latitudinal Cross-Validation

Since our data is neatly partitioned into multiple stock symbols, it is easy to create an out-of-sample performance simulation of our machine learning model by simply separating the stock symbols into two separate sets. Readers are encouraged to do so on multi-asset strategies, in general, as it provides an easy method for performing out-of-sample performance tests on any type of strategy.

Further, the cross-validation method presented in this chapter can be modified to split labels along stock symbols if it is made aware of the symbol of each label. This could be a potentially useful method for discovering true patterns in market activity across symbols.

Cursory tests show that the model presented in this chapter does not hold up to latitudinal out-of-sample testing, and underperforms the S&P 500 in simulation, suggesting that it is an overfit resulting from data leakage within single symbols.

7.8 Conclusion

In this chapter, we developed a financial machine learning pipeline with a lot of the core accouterments that differentiate it from a normal machine learning pipeline. We also discovered that it is a non-trivial problem to predict investment outcomes even when we have a reasonably good idea about revenue as it is earned as opposed to as it is reported. This, in itself, might have some philosophical implications for what it means to be a good investor in the 21st century. It may be that only accurate forward-looking predictions of revenue generation provide an informational advantage in the market, or it may be that more contextual information is needed about a company before a significant model can be devised.

CPSIA information can be obtained
at www.ICGtesting.com
Printed in the USA
LVHW021737240723
753297LV00011B/723